WOMEN, RESILIENCE, AND THE WILL TO LEAD

WOMEN, RESILIENCE, AND THE WILL TO LEAD

Linda Kasonde

Published by Linda Kasonde
•
https://lindakasonde.com/
C/O Chapter One Foundation
Plot 6941 Suez Road
Cathedral Hill
Lusaka 10101
Zambia
•
First published 2023
1 3 5 7 9 8 6 4 2
•

Printed and bound by Tandym Print
•
ISBN 9780796105097

Set in Adobe Caslon Pro 11pt

This book is dedicated to my mum, Dorothy; my dad, Joseph; my sister, Mubanga, "Bangs"; my brother, Mutale, "Tal"; –thank you for always being there for me.

To my niece and nephews, Kalela, Joseph, and Mukuka; know that there is no limit to what you and the women in your life can do.

About the author

Linda Kasonde is a lawyer and a civil rights activist. She is the owner and founder of LCK Chambers and is also the founder and Executive Director of Chapter One Foundation, an organisation that promotes human rights and the rule of law in Zambia. Linda was admitted to the Zambian Bar in 2001. She holds an LLB Law from the University of Leicester and an LLM from the University of Cape Town.

Prior to setting up LCK Chambers and Chapter One Foundation, Linda worked in one of the most well-recognised commercial law firms in Zambia for fifteen years earning the position of named Partner. She is a member of the Chartered Institute of Arbitration (MCIarb). She is the first woman to be elected as President of the Law Association of Zambia in the history of the Bar Association in Zambia. Linda has written a memoir about her experiences as a woman in leadership in Zambia between 2011-2021 trying to challenge creeping authoritarianism in Zambia.

Linda has undergone several leadership fellowships and programmes including the Stanford University Draper Hills Fellowship, the Archbishop Desmond Tutu Leadership Fellowship, the US State Department's International Visitor Leadership Programme (IVLP), the UK's Foreign and Commonwealth and Development Office's International Leaders Programme (ILP), and the Harvard University Leadership in the 21st Century programme. Linda has received both local and international recognition for her leadership including as a 2017 recipient of the IE University's Extraordinary People Inspiring the IE Community (EPIC) Award in the 'Women Inspiring Women' category. In December 2016, the prestigious The Africa Report named her as one of the people to watch out for in 2017 in Southern Africa. Linda is also the Vice-President for Africa of the Commonwealth Lawyers' Association and formerly a member of the Advisory Board of the Africa Regional Forum and the Bar Issues Commission of the International Bar Association.

To learn more about Linda, please visit her website:

https://lindakasonde.com/

CONTENTS

Foreword

I first met Linda, in person, when she was serving as the first female President of the Law Association of Zambia, and I was leading a civil society organisation. We both were not too popular with the then-government because of our advocacy work. No, Linda and I did not meet at yet another what-shall-we-do-to-respond-to-a-new-abrogation-of-the-law-by-powerholders CSO meeting. She invited me for coffee at a café. I accepted, expecting to talk shop and only shop. We didn't. We spoke about all manner of topics. From that day we went from being two women in the public eye in Zambia, virtual colleagues, to mutual sounding boards, escapes from the demands of our work, and good friends. That is Linda! A proactive, generous, human.

I was glad when she told me she was writing a book. Firstly, because I knew that it would fill the huge gap of insider protagonists' perspectives in the various eras of Zambian civil and political life. While Zambia's history has, to a significant extent, been influenced by civic actors who have held fort when much seemed threatened in the life of the nation, not much is known of what happened to the individuals involved behind closed doors. Unfortunately, few who had a front row seat or field of play in the strategizing, hair-pulling, and execution of civic activism have recorded their experiences for posterity.

Secondly, this book is important simply because it sets out the personal story, world view, and experiences of a leader who made her mark on Zambia. Linda chooses to think of herself as a female leader and presents her story as such. I argue that she is one of the most influential individuals of her generation – male or female. What this book shows is that every leader was once a little girl or boy who walked a path, never quite easy, to prominence.

I encourage the reader to enjoy this book of a tale of a contemporary leader, a member of a close-knit family, and a woman who has placed an indelible footprint on our recent history.

Laura Miti, 18th June 2023

PREFACE

In April 2016, I was elected as the first female President of the National Bar Association, the Law Association of Zambia. I would like to believe that my tenure was significant not just because I was the first woman to hold the position on a national stage, but also because I challenged many preconceptions of women's ability to lead in a tough political environment. I wanted to write a book that not only narrates my experiences as a woman in leadership, but also talks about why it is important. So often the debate around the need for gender equality or equity is centred around the need to have more women in positions of influence, but neglects to make the case for why it isn't just a case of making up the numbers. About a decade ago, I heard the then-Swedish Foreign Minister on the BBC World Service illustrate the point very nicely. She told the story of two warring factions fighting over a river on a map. At the time, there were only men at the discussion table. She narrated how when women were finally brought into the conversation, they pointed out that in fact, the river that the men were fighting over had dried up many years ago. They knew this because women in that community bore the responsibility of drawing water for their families. The truth is that women have different lived experiences from men and therefore have different perspectives on life from their male folk.

One of the greatest myths perpetuated by society is that all women are the same; and yet, individually, their experiences, attitudes, and even behaviours, are also varied. In my career, I have found that women in positions of influence face biases such as the perception that all women should be "soft", "motherly", and "humble". If by some "cruel" twist of fate, you do not happen to fit into that archetype, you are perceived to be unwomanly, if not manly. That makes you a target for cyberbullying and other unfortunate attempts to diminish you and your achievements. Often, women experts are overlooked in favour of men. And because so few women are recognised as being experts in their field, it reinforces society's belief that there just are no women to pick from. You will find them if you deliberately look for them – and yes, extra effort is required.

There is a widely held belief in many societies,

including my own, that men are naturally smarter, more competent, and more knowledgeable than women. I grew up in a home in which my sister, my brother, and I were treated equally. We all washed the dishes, made our beds, and learnt how to cook. I played football at school and my parents never suggested that that was not appropriate for girls, nor did they ever suggest that boys were cleverer or more competent than girls – that certainly was not my lived experience.

In March 2022, I attended a Women's Day conference as a panellist. During the plenary, one woman raised her hand and said, "We attend Women's Day events every year; how can we take the conversation forward?" I responded that in fact women have the greatest ability to break the gender bias every day by how they raise their children. As someone once said, "Good parenting is the greatest form of activism." Perhaps some women may have taken offence at a childless woman telling them how to raise their kids. I certainly am no expert on raising kids, but I believe that how I was raised definitely shaped my worldview on gender equity.

Because men are socialised to be leaders and women are socialised to remain in the background, it can be harder to find women to fill leadership roles, especially in politics. But the challenge is not insurmountable. Deliberate efforts must be made to identify female talent. Sometimes, a little more coaxing and reassurance are required. For example, in public discussions, you will find that men are very quick to pose questions to the panellists; they may not even put up their hands before doing so. Women, on the other hand, are much more reluctant to speak up. When faced with such a situation as either a moderator or panellist, I deliberately ask and encourage women to speak up. Expecting men and women to be equally assertive when they are socialised differently is simply to ignore the realities of our socialisation.

But equally, women are sometimes reluctant to put themselves forward because society has told them that men are better than them. Even I struggle with this sometimes. Last year, I was organising a workshop and one of our male speakers dropped out. I actually had to convince myself that the work that I currently do qualifies me as an expert able to replace him. This scenario is called the Imposter Syndrome and it has got to stop. Ladies, representation matters, and we need you to step up. You are enough!

CHAPTER ONE

IT MATTERS HOW IT STARTS

"Let's start from the very beginning, a very good place to start."

– Fräulein Maria in *The Sound of Music*[1]

I was born in Zambia in the late 1970s under the Kenneth Kaunda regime. Six years previously, the country had changed from a multi-party democracy into a one party "participatory" democracy. Over the years Kaunda, a well-respected Pan-Africanist and champion of independence movements across Africa, had begun to rule with an iron fist. Zambia was home to one of the best intelligence services on the continent and there was a palpable fear of being monitored. I recall being told not to say certain things over the phone or around certain people.

I finally met the great man when I was about six years old. As a result of my mother being Kaunda's wife's physician, our family had been invited to the State House for his daughter's wedding reception. During the reception we lined up to congratulate the newlywed couple. Kaunda himself was in the receiving line. When I got to him, I held out my little hand and genuflected, as per local tradition when greeting elders, as I shook his right hand. He put his left hand on my head and began to push me down to the floor, wanting me instead to greet him from a kneeling position. At first, I resisted, but his hand was very strong. I succumbed, kneeling in greeting for the next few people in the line before I got up. I will never forget the feeling of being forced into submission. I understood his power quite differently from that point on.

By the time we got into the late 1980s, our country's fortunes were changing, and the economy began to crumble. Kaunda began to lose his grip on power as our economic woes continued. A new movement for the reintroduction of multi-party democracy emerged in which my father played a small part by supporting the leaders of the movement as they sought to spread their message from the mining towns of the Copperbelt into Lusaka, the capital of Zambia. By 1990, Kaunda was forced to call for early elections, which were held in 1991 under a new Constitution. Kaunda was resoundingly defeated.

When the new Movement for Multi-party Democracy (MMD) came into power, we were told that our economic woes would continue for some time and that we all needed to "tighten our belts" and "bite the bullet" as the economy was being restructured through the IMF's structural adjustment programme. This message was delivered by my Uncle Emmanuel when he was the Minister of Finance. No Zambian family was spared the effects of the economic downturn; inflation soared, and interest rates reached triple digits. Our family narrowly avoided our house being repossessed. In the midst of stringent exchange controls and high inflation rates, my sister and I were sent to boarding school in Swaziland, now called Eswatini. I hated boarding school, but it played a critical role in developing my worldview.

I had started my education at Lake Road Primary School, which at the time was a very good school. It was a multi-racial, multi-ethnic, and multi-religious school. The owner of the school, an Irish woman, was very frugal with the infrastructure at the school and it was not until the management changed decades later that someone thought to grow grass on the barren playground.

During my primary school days, we lived next door to the Chiumyas. They were friends of our parents and we in turn became friends with their children. My sister was a year older, and I was a year younger than their middle child, Natasha, with whom we spent many delightful afternoons playing games like hopscotch, chicken in the den, and hide-and-seek; or playing board games like Monopoly, Snakes and Ladders, and Cluedo. We would also put on plays and musical performances for our parents, who were our clients and who subsequently had to pay for the refreshments that we served them from their own pantries. The Chiumyas also had a wide collection of videos classic children's musicals. We spent endless hours rewatching *The Sound of Music*, *Mary Poppins*, and *Chitty Chitty Bang Bang*. To this day, I can still recite the lyrics.

I went to boarding school in Swaziland at age eleven. It was also a multi-racial, multi-religious school. Our school was named Waterford Kamhlaba, "Kamhlaba" meaning "one world" in the native Siswati language. The school was established in response to apartheid in neighbouring South Africa. Many anti-apartheid activists had sent their children there, including Nelson Mandela. Alongside the usual school subjects, sports and community service were mandatory. Our school was also visited by many anti-apartheid activists who shared their stories with us. In many ways, that experience shaped the person that I was to become.

Boarding school was an unhappy experience for me as a socially awkward and introverted child, but it made me become very independent and resilient, traits that would later allow me to make unconventional and even unpopular decisions in my leadership roles. A chance conversation that I had with a fellow student in the first year of my International Baccalaureate Diploma would forever change how I viewed myself as a leader. Elections for the Student Representative Council had come around again and traditionally the SRC was headed by members of the IB1 class. A classmate of mine, Kwaku, asked me if I was standing for any position on the SRC and I replied that I was not standing because I did not think anyone would vote for me. "That's a lousy attitude!" he told me. It stung, but at the time I felt completely justified in my opinion; after all, the elections were essentially a popularity contest, and I did not consider myself to be popular; I was quiet and shy. This conversation had a lasting impression on me.

I graduated from Waterford with an International Baccalaureate Diploma at the end of 1996. In the preceding months, my Welsh boyfriend had helped me make applications to various British universities as I had expected to go to university in the United Kingdom. I had no fixed career ambitions at the time. My mother had always told my sister and me that, as women, it was important to have a profession because whatever happened to you, you would always have that thing to fall back on.

History and English had long been my favourite subjects. My father had always thought that I would become a journalist because I loved to write poems and short stories. I opted for law as a "respectable" profession, not having had any personal interaction with any lawyers whilst growing up. Looking back, the only trait I can associate with any inclination towards the law was my tendency to ask a lot of questions and defend the underdog in any argument. When I got home from Swaziland, my parents told me that I would not be going to the United Kingdom as I had hoped but would instead be going to the University of Zambia to do my law degree. They reasoned that if I wanted to practise law in Zambia, it would be a good idea to have a network of local peers with whom I could engage and consult. I, on the other hand, was not thinking that far ahead. I was extremely disappointed, not least because I had hoped to reunite with my boyfriend in England.

The University of Zambia, or UNZA, as it is

otherwise known, has a proud history of producing some of Zambia's finest minds. My mother would narrate stories of how when she was there, the government would pay for lavish meals, how students' linen was changed by housekeepers, and how their subsistence allowance would allow them to purchase clothes and other items. By the time I got to UNZA, the university had been run down considerably. The facilities left much to be desired. However, as one of two public universities at the time, it still had the reputation of only accepting the best and the brightest in the country. To get into UNZA one had to achieve at least twelve points at Grade 12 from your six best subject scores, an A1 being the highest score. To get into law school, after the first year of university, one had to attain a certain level of grades that only a few students would obtain. Law was seen as an elite course. Because I had done my International Baccalaureate Diploma, which was two years of education post Form Five, and because I had the grades, I was able to go straight into law school.

I was immensely impressed by the studiousness of the students at UNZA who hit the library almost as soon as we started class. The class consisted of about forty students, all very bright and eager to learn. Three weeks into my time at UNZA, just as I was settling in, the university students went on strike. During that time and in preceding years, UNZA strikes were known to be prolonged, often extending a four-year course into a six-year one. My parents assessed the situation and decided that I should complete my studies in England after all.

I spent about six months at home before going to university in England. Having lost touch with the friends I went to primary school with over my seven years at boarding school, much of my time was spent alone reading or occasionally accompanying my very socially active sister on her outings. By the time it was time to go back to university in September of 1997, I was very ready to go. I settled on the University of Leicester, which was located in the English Midlands – away from expensive London and far enough away from the colder northern part of England.

Leicester was a pleasant town known for its greenery, pies, and potato crisps. I enjoyed taking long walks from the university into the city centre in its leafy streets. I was provided accommodation by the university. It was amazingly comfortable and generally clean. Having been in boarding school for the previous seven years, the allure of local students' newfound "freedom" to go for pub crawls was lost on me. I eventually made friends with a small group of first-year students from Kenya and Tanzania,

Diane, Nasra, and Cheri. Luckily for me, my cousin Chisanga was also at Leicester University, and Qochiwe, a Malawian friend and fellow classmate from Waterford, was at the neighbouring De Montfort University. My university days were some of the best days of my life with my friends and me oscillating between being footloose and carefree, and trying to stay on top of our schoolwork. We went out dancing: eighties night at the student union, R&B clubs, and sometimes travelled to other towns to have fun.

University was harder than I thought it would be. I barely scraped a pass in some of my subjects in my first year, which came as a shock to me, having been used to getting mostly As in my subjects. By the second year, I had hit my stride. I discovered the subject that changed how I viewed the law; it was called Civil Liberties. It was taught by Professor Peter Cumper, whose experience growing up in troubled Northern Ireland influenced his teaching. It began my interest in human rights law as it again appealed to my natural instincts to protect the underdog and downtrodden, something that I felt I could relate to, having spent many years as a loner.

Throughout my time at Leicester, I was an average student at best. I graduated with a law degree in July of 2000 still none the wiser as to what I wanted to do with my life. I wanted to stay in England but, not having obtained a training contract with an English law firm, qualifying as either a Barrister or a Solicitor would be very difficult. My parents managed to talk me into coming back home, where they were sure I would have better prospects. They were right.

A day after I got home, I was enrolled in the Bar course at the Zambia Institute for Advanced Legal Education, otherwise known by its acronym, ZIALE. At the time I went to ZIALE, almost all the students were UNZA graduates. As a result of having studied in England and avoiding the UNZA strike, I was now in a class with students who were a year ahead of my classmates at UNZA and were a good two to ten years older than me.

There were only forty students in the class. My ZIALE classmates, like my UNZA classmates, were very studious. The Executive Director of ZIALE was an irrepressible woman called Mrs. Mukelebai who gave us daily reminders of the consequences of not studying hard enough. She was also very strict about the attire that students wore; we were lawyers and had to look the part. White or blue shirts with a dark grey, navy blue, or black suit, and heels for the women. You could be sent home if you were not properly dressed. Mrs. Mukelebai also implored the female students not to despise humble beginnings and advised that amongst the male students were potentially very eligible bachelors. If I had not been so young, at twenty-one, and totally burnt out from jumping from one stressful exam experience to another, I might have seen her point.

ZIALE classes took place in the afternoons. In the morning, we were expected to gain work experience at a law firm. The first firm I worked for was run by a sole practitioner who had been recommended to me by Mrs. Mukelebai. He was a serious man who appeared to find my presence an inconvenience. Often, I had no work to do and would have to ask for something to do, which was grudgingly assigned. I left out of sheer boredom and the fear that I would not gain the required experience. I ended up at a more established firm with its roots on the Copperbelt that had just set up an office in Lusaka. It was run by the Managing Partner's daughter who, at eight years older than me, seemed very wise and motherly. I worked there until the end of my ZIALE. I failed three of the ten exams I sat in the finals. Given how exhausted I was, I was not too disappointed. The ZIALE exams are notoriously difficult to clear. Modern-day pass rates are at around three per cent on the first attempt. Every year a debate rages as to why the pass rate is so low, with allegations that lawyers are deliberately trying to prevent new entrants from entering the legal profession in a bid to reduce competition.

In my class of 2001, around fifty per cent of the class cleared on the first attempt. I sat my repeater's exams a few months later. As I waited for my results, I signed up in October 2000 to volunteer at a local legal aid clinic in Lusaka called the National Legal Aid Clinic for Women. It was run by a good-humoured man who was a retired army colonel. It was like Charlie's Angels; he was the head of an all-female team. The Clinic provided free legal services to indigent women and children. Most of the cases related to family law: divorce cases, custody, probate, and succession. The women we served were the most vulnerable in our society with heart-wrenching stories of despair and desperation. The work aligned perfectly with my love of human rights. It was important, and for many, life changing.

Although I enjoyed the work, I was somewhat constrained by my lack of fluency in the two main vernacular languages, Nyanja and Bemba. English is the only official language in Zambia. Although Bemba is my mother tongue, I feel much more comfortable using my broken Nyanja. I had grown up with my parents largely speaking to us in English. The first time I realised that I could not understand any vernacular language properly was at primary school in Grade 6. I was about ten years old at the time. Although our school did not forbid the use of vernacular languages, English was the medium most commonly used. One day in class, someone cracked a joke in Nyanja and to my own surprise, I didn't get the joke. I had picked up some Nyanja from playing with the workers' children in the neighbourhood. It was also more comfortable for me to try to communicate in Nyanja to avoid the shame of not being able to speak my mother tongue. The only people with whom I tried to speak Bemba were my grandparents, who did not speak English. Even then, I made sure no one else was around to witness my pitiful lack of fluency. When I was growing up in Lusaka, Nyanja was the lingua franca. Although the words to speak, "*ku kamba*", and to understand, "*ku mvela*", are completely separate and distinct, when people find out that I cannot speak any vernacular language, they immediately assume that I cannot understand any of it. This has led to me overhearing interesting things about myself from people who assume that I cannot understand them.

I got called to the Zambian Bar in December 2001. It was a proud moment for my parents. My dad bought me my first leather briefcase. It was black, smart, and heavy and is still stored in pristine condition. Ours was the last Call Day ceremony presided over by a now-retired Chief Justice who since fell from grace after having been discovered to have taken a bribe from a former head of state. The ceremony itself was a sombre affair borrowing from anachronistic English legal traditions.

Fully licensed to practise, I could now ply my trade anywhere I wanted in Zambia. I chose to stay at the clinic. I continued to work there as a volunteer; I would not be fully employed as an Advocate for several months. The work at the clinic was extremely rewarding and fulfilling, but after three years, my clients' problems had begun to take an emotional toll on me. Every morning we would find dozens of women lined up waiting for legal assistance for social problems that did not always have neat solutions. I started looking for a new job and was told that a small but reputable law firm in the Lusaka city centre was looking to hire. I took in my application and was called for an interview by the two founding partners. I was hired and the firm became my home for the next fifteen years.

I worked hard and long hours at my new job and it soon began to pay off. The firm grew in size and stature, and I grew with it. Just before I turned thirty-one, a good friend of mine, Natasha, urged me to ask the founding partners if I could be made an equity partner. Much to my surprise, the founding partners agreed. I was responsible for managing the administration at the firm and also supervising the Associates, both responsibilities that I enjoyed. My two partners very generously supported my participation in the affairs of the local Bar Association, the Law Association of Zambia, popularly known by its acronym, LAZ.

LAZ is a statutory body mandated to regulate the legal profession in Zambia. It also has a mandate to be a watchdog over national rule of law, human rights, and constitutional issues. There, I found community and a sense of purpose. I volunteered to be on the committees of LAZ, gradually rising to head one of the committees, from which platform I was encouraged to stand for a position on the Council of LAZ, the governing body of the Association, in 2012. I thought back to my conversation with Kwaku at Waterford and this time decided to take the plunge. When the LAZ election results came out, I had the third-highest number of votes for a non-Executive Council member. I came to realise that my earlier fears of not being popular were unfounded. As it turns out, half the battle is just putting yourself out there.

The LAZ Council is made up of four Executive positions: The President, Vice-President, Honorary Secretary, and Honorary Treasurer; and twelve non-Executive Council members. Being a Council member was very engrossing. The President who led us was a young but very seasoned Council member. The atmosphere was collegial. At the time, through practice but also through the personality of our President, there was far more deference given to the LAZ President. In those days, most decisions were made by the Executive Council members who oversaw the day-to-day running of the Association. That came with some frustration on the part of non-Executive Council members.

I continued balancing my work at the firm, gradually performing more of an administrative role than practising law. In 2013, I decided to stand for the executive position of Honorary Secretary of LAZ. I stood because I believed that, for that moment, it was my purpose to serve the Association and the community at large. As an advocate for women's empowerment, I also felt it was important to lead by example. Before making the decision to stand, I consulted a few of my friends, who encouraged me to stand but also warned me that I should be prepared to fail. One of them gave me a book entitled *Dare to Fail* by Billi P.S. Lim. The premise of the book is that one should not be afraid of failure as it is not necessarily an end in itself but an opportunity to learn from and overcome one's mistakes or shortcomings.

Do not get me wrong; I am afraid of failure, but my urge to empower myself and others is greater.

In *Dare to Fail*[2] the author tells the story of a young lady who desperately wanted to become a prima ballerina. She practised regularly and one day heard that a renowned ballet master was coming to her town. She went backstage after the performance and sought an audience with the ballet master. He asked her to dance for him and she did. Afterwards he said, "No, no, no, you don't have what it takes." The young lady went away devastated. She gave up her hopes of becoming a ballerina and instead became a wife and mother. Many years later the same ballet troupe came back to her town, and she went to see the ballet master again. She said to him that it had troubled her all those years that he had dismissed her talent so easily, asking, "How could you tell so easily that I didn't have what it takes?" The master replied that he had barely looked at her and that that was his standard response to all the ballerinas who danced for him. Incredulous, the lady told him that he had ruined her chances of becoming a prima ballerina. He replied, "No, no, if you had what it takes, you wouldn't have paid any attention to what I said." There is a lesson in that story for all of us.

Sheryl Sandberg's book, *Lean In*, has received a lot of publicity and acclaim. In it she challenges women to become influential. I watched her give an interview on CNN's *Leading Women*[3] programme in which she revealed that she still had a lot of the insecurities other women have about taking up leadership positions. Many women do not take up leadership roles because they do not think they are good enough. In her book, Sandberg narrates how Virginia Rometty, IBM's first female CEO, asked that question of herself when considering taking up that position. She told the recruiter that she needed to think about whether she should accept the job. Her husband's response was, "Do you think a man would have ever answered that question that way?" As Sandberg points out, men will put their hand up to do a job that a woman with twice the ability will hesitate over. More women need to lean in.

It is true that risking failure can have devastating and sometimes very public consequences, but what about the potential rewards of trying? As I stated earlier, failure need not be an end in itself. An extreme example is Tiger Woods' spectacular fall from grace, in spite of which he managed to dust himself off and regain his number-one position. I think that is very admirable. Less extreme is the case of Abraham Lincoln. According to Lim, he failed in business in 1831 and 1833; was defeated in the legislature in 1832; had a nervous breakdown in

1836; was defeated in Congress in 1843 and 1848; defeated in the Senate in 1855; defeated in running for Vice President in 1856; and defeated in running for the Senate in 1858 before finally becoming one of the best and most memorable presidents in American history in 1860.

Sheryl Sandberg has a very powerful mantra which she hung up on the walls of the Facebook offices: "What would I do if I wasn't afraid?" I would add another one: "Where would we be if we believed we had what it takes?" As Nelson Mandela once famously said, "Courage is not the absence of fear but the triumph over it."[4] On the morning the nominations for the Law Association of Zambia's elections opened, a friend of mine sent me a text message. She had asked about ten of her friends what they thought of my candidacy and most of them had responded that they were unsure of who I was. She asked me if I was sure I still wanted to stand. For a moment doubt set in but, with the encouragement of another friend, I decided to file my nomination come what may. As I waited anxiously for the results of the election to come in, I realised my moment of reckoning had come. A lot of preparation and canvassing had brought me to that point, but would I be successful? Fortunately, I won by a very convincing margin; I beat my opponent by a ratio of two votes to one. It quite easily could have gone the other way but if I had not tried, I would never have known.

I put my heart and soul into the role of Honorary Secretary. The work was much harder than being a non-Executive Council member. I was responsible for running the LAZ Secretariat, taking the minutes of the Council meetings, which included six scheduled meetings and several extraordinary meetings, and taking the minutes of the weekly Executive Council member meetings, drafting statements, attending courtesy calls, attending to media engagements, sorting through the correspondence, and participating in the decision-making. I worked under the leadership of a veteran LAZ President who gave me a lot of encouragement and responsibility. Through him, I was exposed to the media and learnt how to handle press queries and media interviews. His main tip was to make sure that, in whatever interview you had, you should deliver the message you intend to give to the public, whatever questions are posed to you. I also learnt a lot about politics from him; he was a good teacher. I would ask him for advice even after I left office. He never told me what to do but would always ask the right questions.

My biggest test came in mid-2013 when the LAZ President asked me to read out on national television the resolution of the LAZ Extraordinary

General Meeting calling for the resignation of the Acting Chief Justice Lombe Chibesakunda. Justice Chibesakunda had reached the constitutional retirement age but had continued to serve as the Acting Chief Justice on a contract, which meant that she did not have security of tenure. This meant that her position was more vulnerable to political interference. LAZ had held an extraordinary general meeting on 4th May 2013 which had resolved that Justice Chibesakunda was not qualified to hold the substantive position of Chief Justice and that if engagement with her office and the appointing authority did not work after a reasonable time, we were authorised to litigate over the matter. I had suspected that the LAZ President had passed the buck, unwilling to "do the deed" himself, but I decided that I would do it because it was the right thing to do. I recall a number of people telling me that they thought that I had been "used" to make the statement, but the truth is that I had done so of my own volition. As Honorary Secretary, I was responsible for taking all the minutes and drafting the LAZ press statements, a role which was much easier at that time as only the four Executive Council members would draft and finalise statements. It made things quick and easy but caused a lot of discontent among the other twelve non-Executive

Council members who felt left out of decision-making. In those days, the legal profession was much more united and LAZ members easily rallied around positions taken by LAZ, a situation that would change in the coming years with growing political polarisation.

In April 2014, I was elected Vice-President of LAZ under very controversial circumstances. At the 2013 Annual General Meeting, LAZ had passed a resolution that Executive Council Members had to have a minimum of ten years post-qualification experience to hold office. Under the Law Association of Zambia Act, resolutions of the Annual General Meeting are binding. The resolution was not reduced into a statutory instrument. By April 2014, I had clocked thirteen years of post-qualification experience. My only opponent, Sydney Chisenga, had not yet clocked ten years at the Bar. Upon filing his nomination, Sydney's nomination was rejected by LAZ's Electoral Committee. There was a huge uproar. As a member of the Executive Council of LAZ, I was accused of manipulating the decision in my favour. Sydney took to social media to denounce me. By the time we got to the AGM in April 2014, I had been vilified as a power-hungry despot. Sydney and his team were brewing a motion to place on the AGM floor to allow him to stand. On the eve of the

AGM, the President sent out an addendum to the AGM pack explaining how the situation had arisen and what rules had been applied. As a result, on the day of the AGM, Sydney's motion never materialised. I had scraped my way into office but was very bruised and very unpopular. I decided to put my head down and prove that I was worthy of the position.

At those LAZ elections, George Chisanga was elected as President unopposed. He was a mature, intelligent man, but for the life of him could not keep time. He was connected to the ruling Patriotic Front party, having sought adoption as a Member of Parliament on their ticket in the 2011 general elections. He was not adopted. However, it did lead some sections of the press to label our Council as pro-Patriotic Front. I had been discouraged to stand as Vice-President by my mother, who was the then-Patriotic Front Republican President Michael Sata's personal physician. She and I had had a number of conversations about the stance that LAZ had taken regarding rule of law issues. Some messages were indirectly from President Sata himself. As a professional lawyer, I had learnt to keep personal issues away from business, even though it was an uneasy balancing act at times.

George's style of leadership was more inclusive. In what I suspect was a break from tradition, non-

Executive members of the Council were asked for input on all LAZ statements and decisions in between scheduled meetings. It was cumbersome, but it quelled the discontent that had previously been felt by non-Executive Council members. Communication was made easy by the introduction of the social media app WhatsApp. By default, it became my role to ensure that statements went out on time and that decisions were made in a timely manner. I suspect this is where I gained the unfortunate reputation of bulldozing my way through things. During George's tenure, I was often given the opportunity to chair meetings. I did not mind as it gave me experience, but one episode in particular showed me the real challenges of stepping up to the plate.

In March 2015, the newly elected President, Edgar Lungu, had appointed Likando Kalaluka as the new Attorney-General. Likando had been elected as Honorary Secretary of LAZ in 2014. His appointment as Attorney-General was subject to ratification by the National Assembly. Traditionally LAZ, as custodians of the legal profession, were invited to make submissions to a select committee of the National Assembly to determine the suitability of the candidate for office. As per tradition, the LAZ Council invited senior lawyers of the rank of State

Counsel to give their views. The majority of the State Counsel did not support the appointment as they felt Likando lacked the requisite experience. After hearing from the State Counsel, a Council meeting was convened to determine the issue. George had excused himself from the meeting having declared a conflict of interest. Likando, as the subject of the deliberations, was equally excused.

It was then left for me to chair the meeting. After some deliberation over the issue, I called for a vote. The votes were tied, six for the appointment and six against. The Law Association of Zambia Act provided that in the event of a tie, the Chair had the casting or deciding vote. I cast my vote against the appointment. A submission to Parliament was crafted, careful not to impugn Likando's character, but clear in the view that it was felt that he lacked the requisite experience to assume the office of Attorney-General. On 21st March 2015, a Canadian-based Zambian lawyer, Elias Munshya, published a scathing attack on LAZ and on me personally for the decision. It was alleged that the decision had been influenced by tribalism and that I had no right to "vote twice"[5]. There was a huge furore about this issue in the media and on social media. It was alleged that I was jealous of Likando because I wanted the position of Attorney-General myself and that I was a tribalist.

It was a very lonely and tough time for me. I had been motivated to do what I thought was the right thing no matter how unpopular. At the parliamentary select committee hearing, I had made it clear that the lack of experience was not on account of his age; after all, his predecessor Musa Mwenye SC had been about the same age when he was appointed but had a greater wealth of depth and experience. Three years later, I read an article by Elias Munshya in which he retracted his views in hindsight. Too late, I thought, the damage had already been done.

I had wanted to be LAZ President at least seven years before I stood for office. I knew that if I wanted to win, I would have to run an extraordinary race. I assembled my team made up of twelve men and women of various levels of seniority at the Bar. They helped spread the word and later gather proxies from LAZ members who would not be able to attend the AGM. I knew of at least one mole who attended the meetings but never said anything. But amongst my team I picked two trusted, young, and streetwise lawyers whom I dubbed "The Fixers" who I would go to about campaign strategy and fixing problems. The election would be held in April 2016.

By November 2015 I was ready to start campaigning. As a Vice-President of LAZ, becoming President ordinarily should have been a natural progression. However, in the entire history of the Bar Association in Zambia, no woman had ever been elected President of LAZ. I was also up against the perception that I had been the "de facto President" under the leadership of the previous LAZ President and therefore that I had already done my time. This was in spite of the fact that previous LAZ Presidents had held the positions for several terms.

There had been three previous attempts by women to stand as LAZ President: Josephine Nyirongo SC, Nelly Mutti, and Kondwa Sakala-Chibiya. Mrs. Nyirongo was much older than me, so I have no recollection of her days in LAZ politics. Mrs. Mutti had stood for election a few months after I was called to the Bar in a heated election which was ultimately won in a proxy war. Michael Musonda emerged victorious after amassing an unprecedented number of proxy votes. This subsequently led to a change in the LAZ electoral rules, limiting the number of proxies any individual could carry to two.

I had worked on Kondwa's campaign in 2011 in which she had stood against Musa Mwenye. She was a great candidate with all the qualities a leader should possess. At the beginning, she was hesitant about sending out flyers touting her achievements, but her team managed to convince her that it was necessary. Things were looking good until we got the AGM.

It was a national election year and Musa's campaign team had managed to paint Kondwa as a supporter of the then-extremely unpopular incumbent candidate, Republican President Rupiah Banda. Musa won by a landslide. He only stayed in office for a few months before landing a job as Solicitor-General in Michael Sata's new government. James Banda, who had previously been the LAZ Vice-President, then filled the vacancy of LAZ President.

I knew that I wanted to run an issue-based campaign. I had a lot of experience participating in LAZ affairs. I had been an active member of at least five different LAZ Committees at various times. I had been a non-executive member of the Council, the Honorary Secretary, and Vice-President of LAZ. But more importantly I had achievements to my name. Some of these were the introduction of the mentorship programme, community service initiatives, leading the organising committee of the LAZ fortieth anniversary celebrations which created the first-ever five-year strategic plan, the legal aid week, the new LAZ logo and motto; brought two highly sought-after international law conferences to Zambia and restructured our website to make it more user-friendly. My two opponents, Sydney Chisenga and Kafula Mwiche, despite having spent a considerable time on the LAZ Council, did not have much in the way of a track record and were running almost entirely on personal popularity. But of course, they were also men. It only became clear to me how implausible electing a female LAZ President appeared when I started campaigning.

One aspect of women in leadership that is often spoken about is how people relate to women in leadership. On a Saturday night during the LAZ campaign period, I sat down to watch the *Let's Talk* programme on ZNBC, which highlighted the successes and challenges of successful women in Zambia. Towards the end of the programme, the presenter posed a question to all three of the ladies being interviewed: "Do women hate other women?" I am sad to say that without exception all three ladies narrated the challenges they had faced with unwarranted negativity from fellow women, what they referred to as the "pull-me-down syndrome". Even sadder is the fact that I could relate to what they were saying.

The very same night that I was watching the *Let's Talk* programme, Thandiwe, a friend of mine, sent me a text message saying that she had just finished reading *Lean In*. In the book, Sandberg urges women to come forward and "sit at the table"[6] of influence. As she was reading it, Thandiwe had thought of me because in the book Sandberg writes about a Harvard study[7] that shows that the higher up women go, the less men and women like them. She asked me how people were receiving the news of my candidacy. I told her that was true that I had experienced some bias on account of me being a woman and I gave her some examples:

1. At the time I was a named partner at the law firm I worked at, someone said, "She's too ambitious; why couldn't she just be satisfied with being a partner, why did she also have to ask to have her name on the door?"
2. When I went to give a talk to a group of law students as I was beginning my election campaign, one male student stood up and told me that the only reason that I had been made Vice-President was because of my gender and not because I had earned it.
3. I gave a speech at the graduation dinner of UNZA Law in 2015. At the time, I was Vice-President of LAZ. I joked with one of the female graduates that I still didn't know what I wanted to be when I grow up. And she told me, "You're the Vice-President of LAZ. I think you're done." For her being the Vice-President was the ceiling on a woman's ambition because no one had shown her that actually being a female president was possible.

4. And my personal favourite, "Does Linda read the Bible? Doesn't she know that men are supposed to be in charge?"

In Zambia, it is not expected for women to lead professional organisations, or even the country. Culturally, men are considered to be the "head" and women the "neck" that turns the head. Many women do not aspire for positions beyond being the deputy of the man in charge. Women are expected to exhibit soft and "motherly" traits. When they defy the natural order of things, they are punished by being labelled with all manner of offensive attributes such as having used "bottom power" to climb the career ladder, being "manly", aggressive, shrill, and not being "wife material". I have been labelled all of these things for daring to believe that I could occupy a role that previously had been the preserve of men.

These views are reinforced by men, and women, who are the gatekeepers of our culture. As Winnie Madikizela-Mandela has been quoted as saying, "*The overwhelming majority of women accept patriarchy unquestioningly and even protect it, working out the resultant frustrations not against men but against themselves in their competition for men as sons, lovers, and husbands. Traditionally the violated wife bides her time and off-loads her built-in aggression on her daughter-in-law. So, men dominate women through the agency of women themselves."*

LAZ is not just a professional club; it has a role in influencing public opinion on national legal issues. With the help of my team, we took our campaign to the public. My first interview was a radio interview on the *My Top 10* radio programme on the highly influential Hot FM hosted by the now-deceased veteran radio personality Zacharia "Zachadocious" Chavula. In that interview I was asked about my top-ten favourite songs which I had arranged in a timeline, and which were all played accordingly. Among the songs played were *The Way You Make Me Feel* by Michael Jackson, a song I had been serenaded to in our primary school playground by Francis, a boy who had had a crush on me. I also sang along to one *Teti*, one of my favourite songs done by the Zambian artist formerly known as Exile. It was a great interview because Zach was a very personable character and at only six years older than me, we had basically lived through the same songs. It was a fun show that gave me an opportunity to show a lighter side to me as I was often viewed as being too serious and unapproachable.

I did a number of other radio and print interviews and also shared a well-designed flyer done by Tambana Phiri, my go-to guy, stating my vision and achievements. We had also decided that I needed new campaign photos. For that I called Malekano Mwanza, then of Fortress studio. We took several photos of me in different outfits, but it was the one iconic photo of me looking radiant sitting down wearing a fuchsia dress that really captured the public's imagination. Years after the LAZ Presidency, I had gained some weight and people would ask me for my bio and photo. I would give them a different photo and they would end up using the one of me in a pink dress that they found on the internet. It is only now that people use more recent photos.

In the few days before the election, the Junior Lawyers Committee had organised the first ever LAZ presidential debate. By all accounts, I did not come out on top in that debate. Sydney performed very well. In my estimation, this was largely due to the fact that he was presenting new ideas or change without really understanding how LAZ actually worked. I was handicapped by the fact that because I had played a dominant role as Vice-President of LAZ, many saw me running for the Presidency as an attempt to get a "third term" in office. Sydney was edging the race and all I could do was try harder.

The LAZ AGM is held in the tourist resort of Livingstone every year. LAZ holds a conference in the two days preceding the AGM. For candidates, this is an opportunity to schmooze and canvass last-minute votes. I do not think I have ever shaken as many hands or smiled as much. But my campaigning was hampered by the fact that I was three months into my first pregnancy, which meant that I was exhausted all the time. The pregnancy was something that I had to conceal. It was hard enough trying to get elected as the first female president; adding pregnancy to the mix appeared to be a reach too far. In the last couple of days, it became clear that this race would be decided by a proxy war and Sydney was winning at that game. On the two evenings before the LAZ election, one of my opponents held a function to win supporters over and was freely buying drinks for LAZ members.

I ran an issue-based campaign; I had no wish to bribe my way into office by plying people with free alcohol. I often joke that I spent K100, or about US$5, on my campaign. That is the amount I gave the gentleman who was rumoured to be carrying the cash for the person rumoured to be the State-sponsored candidate. He asked me for a drink, and I gave him a K100 note. I did not consider it to be bribery because I knew where he stood. I did find it curious that he was eating with both hands. On the day of the vote an issue arose as to whether the

State Advocates would be able to vote in the election because their subscription fees had been paid after the deadline for eligibility to vote had passed.

The Fixers asked if I wanted to raise the issue with the Electoral Committee which determines LAZ's electoral disputes. Often State Advocates would have their trip to Livingstone sponsored by the State to support a particular candidate. On the advice of former LAZ President James Banda, I chose not to. I did not want to win on a technicality again. I did not know what to expect but the closer it got to the announcement of the election results, the calmer I felt. I had surrendered to God's will as I had done all I could.

It seemed to take forever to get to the announcement of the results. The Returning Officer, Abha Patel SC, now a judge, had become masterful at building the suspense and lightening the moment. She had smiled and touched my arm as she entered the room. Was this a sign that I had won? When the results were finally read out, the room exploded. I got hugs from everyone around me. I had beaten my two opponents convincingly; I was elated, and a little disbelieving. I would later discover that The Fixers had pulled off what famously became known as the "proxy shuffle". They had duped Sydney into giving his proxies to my supporters who had voted in my favour. I realised that I did not have an overwhelming majority, which meant that I would need to rally those who had not supported me. Also elected to the Executive Council of LAZ were Vice-President Eddie Mwitwa, Honorary Secretary Sashi Kateka, and Honorary Treasurer Andrew Musukwa. I ended my speech that night with the following words from writer Robin Sharma:

> *"Sometimes you'll be the only one who believes in your dream. DO NOT STOP. The world needs you to model what's possible for the rest of us."*[8]

CHAPTER TWO:

"THE IRON LADY"

"You turn if you want to.
The lady's not for turning."[9]
– Margaret Thatcher

Margaret Thatcher was the first female Prime Minister of the United Kingdom. She also became the longest-serving British Prime Minister of the twentieth century. She was a powerful and often divisive figure known for being determined and uncompromising once she had decided to embark on a particular path. As a result, she was given the moniker "The Iron Lady". When I was elected the first female President of LAZ, not much was expected of me. Initially, I was celebrated just because I was the first woman in the position. But later, after powering through what became one of the most turbulent periods in LAZ's history, and some of the most difficult experiences of my life, I too became known as "The Iron Lady".

I am a Black, African, woman. I live in Zambia, a country in the south-central part of Africa. We are known for the beauty of our country, the warmth of our people, and our rich cultural heritage. We are also a very patriarchal society. My tribe, the Bemba-speaking people of Northern Zambia, have sayings such as, "*umwaume ta chepa*" meaning "a man is never inadequate", and "*ubuchende bwa mwaume tautoba ing'anda*", meaning that a man's infidelity will never break a home. A good woman, on the other hand, is "humble", obedient, and "submissive" – to men. I have long resigned myself to the fact that I am not that woman. I earlier mentioned that I was raised to be independent both in thinking and financially. This has meant that I often go against society's expectations of me.

Soon after I was elected to office as the first woman President of LAZ, I got a call from a gentleman called Kelvin Esiasa, now deceased, who ran an organisation called the Zambia Society for Public Administration (ZSPA). ZSPA wanted to give me an award for being elected the first female President of LAZ. I had to pause to think about it. Was winning an election an achievement in itself? I imagined what US President Barack Obama must have felt when he was awarded the Nobel Peace Prize in 2009, barely one year after being elected to office. I did not want to appear rude by turning down the honour. I was elected to office in April 2016; the award ceremony would be in December 2016. I reasoned that that was plenty of time to prove myself, so I said I would attend the event. Little did I know that the next few months would be like walking through fire.

There was a lot of fanfare after I was elected. I was inundated with messages of goodwill from people I knew and even those I didn't. The Republican President Edgar Lungu, President of the leading opposition political party United Party for National Development Hakainde Hichilema; and the leader of the third leading opposition party, The Movement for Multi-party Democracy, Nevers Mumba, all sent me congratulatory messages. Messages also poured in from around the continent and further afield. Before I had decided to stand, I had had a meeting with the partners at my firm. The Managing Partner was dead set against it. He warned that the period following the general election would be "brutal". As it later turned out, he was not wrong. Ultimately, my partners were worried about how my term in office and the heated political environment would negatively affect the firm's business. As a compromise, I opted to take a six-month sabbatical from the firm, during which time we would assess whether it was tenable for me to continue to work at the firm whilst being LAZ President. I subsequently became the first LAZ President to perform the role full time. My partners were kind enough to give me an allowance during my sabbatical. For me LAZ work was something that I was so passionate about that I would have done it for free, but of course, I had bills to pay.

I jumped into my new role with gusto. One of the first things I did was to meet up with my former opponent, Sydney Chisenga, to exchange notes. He had presented some interesting ideas during his campaign, and I wanted to see if there was anything that I could learn from him. One of the things that I had campaigned on was to improve communication with the members. Sydney suggested that we introduce a newsletter, which we subsequently did. We also improved the website and repackaged the information sent out on the mailing list. One of my top priorities was to improve the transparency of the Association. Soon after I returned to Lusaka from the AGM in Livingstone, I bumped into a young lawyer whose proxy my team had courted. She had told a member of my campaign team that she was going to vote for Sydney. When she saw me, she grinned widely and said, "We did it!" This was my first encounter with the fickle nature of "politics". It wouldn't be my last.

I was three months pregnant when elected to office. I had hidden the pregnancy from all but a handful of trusted people because like millions of women before me, I did not think that I would get the job if people knew. Inevitably, my pregnancy began to show, and I embraced it. Thankfully, it did not become a source of public media discussion. Until you get pregnant, no one really explains what it is like .and how your body begins to change. There is also an assumption that you will carry the baby to term and produce a healthy baby. During my first trimester, I was tired all the time but thankfully not nauseous. In the first few months of my term in office, there was much excitement about my election. I was a novelty, a unicorn that the media were very much interested in.

The year I got elected was a national election year. The incumbent, President Edgar Lungu, had "inherited" the reins of power from President Michael Sata who died in office on 28th October 2014. Many Patriotic Front members and indeed some sections of society believed that Edgar Lungu was the "anointed one" who should take over. Lungu ended up winning the presidential by-election held three months after the death of President Sata. On his inauguration day on 25th January 2015, President Lungu announced that he would gift the nation the new Constitution that they had been calling for. President Michael Sata had promised Zambians a new Constitution within ninety days of his election. By the time he died three years later, the new Constitution had not materialised. Civil society had been pushing for a "people-driven" Constitution adopted through a national referendum to ensure that the people's will was not manipulated by politicians as it had been on the previous four occasions that the Constitution had been reviewed.

Interestingly, ahead of the 2015 presidential by-election, the ruling Patriotic Front President was the only presidential candidate of the main political parties who refused to sign the "social contract" prepared by civil society pledging to enact a new people-driven Constitution. In January 2016, the Constitution Amendment Act No. 2 of 2016 was passed, making sweeping amendments to the Constitution outside of the Bill of Rights. It was largely in conformity with what the public had demanded under the last constitutional review process. Fortunately, it appeared that the ruling Patriotic Front party had not fully considered the implications of the amendments that had been made to the Constitution. It would later prove to be part of their undoing.

The next general election would be held on 11th August 2016. President Lungu was extremely popular at the time. He was seen as the guy Zambians could have a drink with, one of them. It soon became apparent that his favourite tipple, Jameson whiskey, was more than just a casual indulgence. At the beginning of his second term in office, it appeared that Lungu could do no wrong for many citizens, but soon troubling signs began to appear.

In May 2016, Parliament was dissolved three months ahead of the August 2016 general election. As per constitutional provision, all members of Parliament were required to vacate their seats, which were tied to the life of Parliament. As all Ministers held their office by virtue of being members of Parliament, they too had to vacate office. This ensured that Ministers would not abuse the advantage of incumbency and government resources to win an election. The Ministers refused to leave office. On 10th May 2016, LAZ issued a statement announcing that it would go to the newly created Constitutional Court to sue all Ministers and Deputy Ministers for failing to leave office following the dissolution of Parliament. This was my first test as the leader of LAZ.

There was a huge backlash from the public and the ruling party against LAZ once it filed its case in the Constitutional Court in May 2016. LAZ had retained the services of renowned constitutional lawyer John Sangwa SC, who was known for not backing down in the face of a challenging fight. However, LAZ was the face of the case and bore the brunt of the ridicule and contempt thrown at us for daring to believe that we could win such a case. I personally received much vilification calling into question my intelligence and competence. In one publication[10], ruling party official Sunday Chanda called me "Legally Blonde" after the seemingly ditsy lead character of the film of the same name.

By month five of my pregnancy, around June 2016, it became apparent that something was wrong. I was bleeding intermittently and had gained more weight than was normal due to water retention. Unsatisfied with the lack of information from my doctor, I made the lifesaving move of changing doctors. It turned out that I had a high-risk pregnancy. I had placenta praevia, a condition in which the placenta sits on the cervix, making it more susceptible to rupture at any time, which could lead to one bleeding to death if the blood was not replaced quickly. I also had HELLP syndrome, a severe form of preeclampsia that causes extremely high blood pressure in pregnant women and can cause seizures pre- and post-delivery. It meant that I had to go on complete bed rest.

For the first few weeks of bed rest, I ran the Association from my bed, organising meetings and events and keeping tabs on what was going on politically. Eventually, on medical advice, I had to stop as my blood pressure remained high. At six and a half months, I was hospitalised after a major bleed and remained there on bed rest, suffering the indignity of using a bed pan and being at the mercy of my carers. On 5th August 2016, at exactly twenty-eight weeks, my placenta ruptured, and I began to bleed profusely. I had to go for an emergency caesarean section to save me and my baby. As I was wheeled into theatre, amazingly quite calm, I prayed that we would be saved.

I woke up a few hours later in the surgical recovery room naked save for the sheet covering my modesty. I was upbeat; I was alive and so was the baby. I had been saved largely due to my new doctor having saved blood for me after our first appointment two months previously. As I was wheeled to my ward, I began to feel some extreme pain in my abdomen. I was undressed and surrounded by several bewildered nurses and doctors. My mother, who is a medical doctor, had noted that my blood pressure had become low. Eventually a nurse pressed my stomach and out popped a blood clot the size of a football. I immediately felt relief.

In Bemba, when a woman delivers a baby safely, she is greeted with the words *Mwapusukeni mukwai* or "You've made it". I had never had to think about how profound those words are. They recognise the perilous nature of childbirth. According to UNICEF's current statistics,[11] the maternal mortality rate in Zambia is around 252 deaths per 100,000 live births. According to a 24th February 2022 press release by Relief Web,[12] Zambia has reduced the maternal mortality rate by 300 per cent since 2002. That is an impressive reduction, however, more needs to be done to save mothers' lives; every life is precious. I survived my ordeal because I could afford the best healthcare on offer. Millions of mothers in Zambia do not have access to adequate healthcare facilities because they live too far away from the facility, or the facility is not adequately staffed and/or stocked with medical supplies.

I was moved to the maternity ward to recover. I had lost a lot of blood and needed several blood transfusions. The catheter that had been inserted in my bladder pre-operation caused an infection of the blood called sepsis. That meant that I had to go on a severe course of intravenous antibiotics. For weeks I excreted blood in my urine. My liver had also taken a beating from the HELLP syndrome. The normal range for D-Dimer, or clotting factor, is 220 to 500ng/mL; mine was at 3000 ng/mL. This meant that I was at risk of having a pulmonary embolism or a stroke.

Since my emergency C-section on 5th August 2016, I had not been able to check on my baby. I would ask after him and my mother and partner would go and check on him. On the morning of 7th August 2016, I asked my partner how my baby was. He looked like he did not know how to respond. From the look on his face, I knew it was bad news. I do not remember who actually told me that my baby had died. A nurse wheeled me to the incubator where he lay peacefully "sleeping". Accompanied by my partner and my mum, I was asked if I wanted to hold him. I held him for a few minutes. He had no clothes on because as he was born prematurely, I had not been ready with baby clothes. He had a full head of hair and was perfectly formed but cold and lifeless. Before he was born, we had named him Mazuba which means sunshine in Tonga, a language from the Southern Province of Zambia where my partner hailed from. Mazuba was only two days old and was no more. I gave him back to the nurse and asked to be wheeled back to my room.

It is true that babies born of mothers with one let

alone both of my conditions had a slimmer chance of survival, particularly if they had not gained enough weight at birth. However, I had been admitted to a private hospital that did not have ventilators for premature babies. I believe he would have stood a better chance at the right hospital with the right facilities. At the time, in Zambia, only the largest hospital in the country's capital, the University Teaching Hospital (UTH), had infant ventilators. Even then, the number of incubators was nowhere near sufficient to meet the demand. It is only one of the reasons why there is such a high infant mortality rate in Zambia. According to UNICEF,[13] the 2016 neonatal infant mortality rate was just over twenty-seven deaths per 1000 live births. That is still quite high, even though the number of deaths has reduced significantly since the 1970s. According to 2021 World Bank statistics,[14] Zambia has a high fertility rate of around 4.3 babies per woman. Losing a baby is treated as something a mother should immediately move on from and have another as though babies are commodities. Some women do not have the luxury of having another one. No baby is replaceable. In our culture, talking about the loss is not encouraged. Many women are not told where their babies have been buried. Some like mine are incinerated. It is a lonely road for many women and not till I had experienced it and talked to a few women who had experienced it did I know how cruel it is.

When I got back to my room, all traces of the congratulatory cards and flowers had been removed. I got into my bed and cried. I cried for two days straight. On the second day, the nurse told me to stop it, otherwise I would get sick. One well-meaning nurse told me that strong women don't cry. I wanted to punch her in the face. As it happened, I did get sicker; the infection in my blood set in and I became very ill. Because my liver was damaged, I also wasn't producing enough blood platelets and needed several more blood transfusions. There was one night in particular when I almost died. The hospital had run out of the stores of my blood type, and I needed more transfusions. My mother, who took the night shift by my bedside, looked scared. She organised some blood from UTH. It literally saved my life.

On 8th August 2016, I was informed that the Constitutional Court had ruled in favour of LAZ in the case in which LAZ had sued all the Ministers and Deputy Ministers for failing to leave office after the dissolution of Parliament. The Court had gone further to order that the Ministers and Deputy Ministers pay back all the emoluments that they had earned while they were illegally in office. Suddenly, the media had moved from calling me "Legally

Blonde" to the "Iron Lady" after the moniker given to former British Prime Minister Margaret Thatcher. It was a bittersweet victory. The national general elections were held on Thursday 11th August 2016. I had registered to vote but while the spirit was willing, my body simply was not well enough to cast my ballot. Another blow, as I had fully intended to demonstrate my displeasure with the incumbent President and his government.

A few days later, I was moved to a larger room to continue my recovery. I was still in the maternity ward which meant I could hear the wailing of other mothers' healthy babies. It was a terribly torturous experience. I remained in that ward for two weeks. At some point during that time, I began to experience the involuntary jerking of my limbs. Because of the possibility of having a seizure due to the HELLP syndrome, I was put on a twenty-four-hour round of hourly injections to prevent a seizure from happening. The injection burned like hell. By the time I was recovering from my last shot, the next one was due. To top it off, there were two nurses who would administer the injection alternately. One of the nurses was kind and gentle. She would inject the drug slowly and soothe my arm as she was doing it. The other nurse just injected me directly and roughly. It was too much to bear. After several rounds of the injection, I had to wake my mum up to tell her to stop the evil nurse from giving me shots. Thankfully, my mum listened to me and intervened. It is important to mention that even in private hospitals in Zambia, one needs a family member to be by their bedside and to be their advocate. It can sometimes be the difference between life and death and was the case for me with my mother, who luckily is also a medical practitioner. I owe my life to her.

When I was discharged, I went home to my mum's. I still had to take injections to reduce the chance of blood clots and continued on the medication to address my hypertension. My mother believes that I had a minor stroke at some point. My tongue was heavy and one of my legs dragged a bit as I walked. I was sad that my baby had died and fell into a deep post-partum depression. I also could no longer stand the sight of my partner who, to his credit, had .sat by my bedside every day that I was in hospital. In retrospect, I believe that that was caused by post-traumatic stress disorder, but I have never received an official diagnosis for it. My relationship fell apart and eventually ended. Thankfully, both before, during, and after my stay in hospital, I was visited by my friends, who made my burden lighter. I told my sister, who lives in London, that I needed her. She came for a few weeks and was also a great source of comfort to me.

On 15th August 2016, the incumbent President Edgar Lungu was declared the President-elect in the 2016 general elections. The January 2016 constitutional amendments had introduced a 50% +1 threshold for winning an election. According to the official results, President Edgar Lungu had 50.35% of the vote compared to the 47.67% attained by Mr. Hakainde Hichilema, his nearest rival. It meant that the country was split down the middle and along regional lines. The tension was palpable in the country and Mr. Hichilema refused to accept the results. He launched a petition in the Constitutional Court challenging the Presidential results. The best and brightest State Counsel joined the case on both sides. LAZ's application to join the case as an amicus curae or friend of the court, was thrown out. A member of the LAZ Council told me that one State Counsel who had represented President Lungu in the case had chided, "Where is your President?" He knew full well where I was as he had made an unexpected visit to my hospital room while the case was on.

The case was plagued by procedural issues that ate into the fourteen-day period provided by the Constitution. There was some confusion as to whether the fourteen-day period provided was for the case to be heard and determined or whether it was simply to hear the arguments and evidence in the case with a judgement delivered at a later date. In a controversial decision, the Constitutional Court reversed an earlier decision allowing the Petitioners more time to present their case. The case was dismissed because the Concourt determined that the Petitioners had run out of time to present their case. A most unsatisfactory result which received a lot of negative press both locally and internationally.

About the end of August 2016, I received a call from a friend and former President of LAZ. He told me that the vultures were circling and that, because of my absence, my presidency was under threat. Still unwell, I had to pull myself together and get back to work.

On my first day back at the LAZ office, my mum and I took a picture to mark the occasion. I had managed to fit into my pre-baby clothes and still had the pregnancy glow. My hair was still thick and lustrous. My hairdressers had warned that, now that I had delivered the baby, my hair would start to fall out, just as my glow would begin to fade. Due to the threat of seizures, I was unable to drive for a couple of months. The LAZ drivers took me to and from the office in the official LAZ vehicles which had our logo stuck on both the front doors. It meant that I could only go to and from work, which made me increasingly socially isolated.

My first day was hard. I had to deal with the awkwardness of people at the office not knowing what to say. It took a while for my liver function to return to normal which meant that I tired easily. The first meeting we had was with State Counsel in September 2016. Only two of them showed up, one of them being the State Counsel who had asked where I was during the presidential election petition. As I entered the room, I could hear him say that he thought that I should resign my position in view of my circumstances. "Hello State Counsel", I said. "I heard you were looking for me; here I am." Needless to say, it was a very awkward meeting.

One of the first things that I did when I got back to the office was to announce my presence. Following Sydney Chisenga's advice, we had introduced the first ever LAZ newsletter. It was meant to inform the membership of our activities and of members' achievements. I would write the editorial while I was in office. For the 26th September 2016 edition of the newsletter, I wrote as follows:

> *"FROM THE PRESIDENT'S DESK*
> *I have been away for the last two months, unwell and recovering from a medical procedure. I would like to thank all those who stepped in for me, sent me gifts and messages of encouragement. I am*

pleased to report that I have recovered just in time for this edition of the newsletter. The purpose of the newsletter is to inform the membership of activities and developments in the Association. The Council still hears some members saying that LAZ seems more concerned with external affairs than the interests of its members. We hear you and want to assure you that there are things that we are working on for your direct benefit. We have realised that we could do a better job of communicating what is being done behind the scenes so, starting with this edition, we are making a conscious effort to inform you of developments that have a direct bearing on you. Having said that, I would like to repeat my calls to you to participate in the affairs of the Association…

My culture has long recognised the difficulties of pregnancy and the perils of childbirth. When a mother safely delivers her child, people will say to her, Mwapusukeni mukwai meaning 'you've survived' or 'you've made it. Similarly, once the election campaign period commenced, the nation was in an expectant state waiting to see who our new leaders will be. This election will go down as one of the most, if not the most, acrimonious election that we have ever had. As a watchdog body, LAZ had a statutory duty to ensure that the elections were conducted in line with the rule of law and constitutionalism, both of which tend to get in the way of politics. As the two main parties battled it out, propaganda became the order of the day with misinformation, innuendo and even lies being spread by both sides. LAZ has not been spared by this unfortunate vice. For example, having read a national broadsheet falsely declaring that during my career I had worked at MNB (now Nchito and Nchito), I now know for sure that you cannot believe everything that you read – even in the mainstream media. Our LAZ Executive was labelled as having sided with the main opposition party and having been part of 'The Cartel'. Nothing could be further from the truth. In fact, in this day and age of polarised mainstream media and social media, honesty seems to be becoming a rare commodity, which is a sad indictment of the moral fabric of our society…

After what was a long wait, we finally have a Republican President in office. LAZ has sent a congratulatory message to his Excellency President Edgar Chagwa Lungu on his re-election. We hope that he will take steps to promote peace and to unite the country, which has become so divided. We wish him all the best during his tenure and look forward to working with the government to ensure that the rule of law and constitutionalism are upheld and to ensure that Zambians can attain justice through the courts of law and through the laws passed by parliament. Following the election period, Zambians appear to now appreciate the need for a new Bill of Rights and for the Constitution to be refined to make it clearer, and we will certainly play a part in those efforts. Now that the elections are over, we can all finally get on with the business of living. 'Twapusuka" –we've made it'."

CHAPTER THREE:

THE QUEST TO SAVE ZAMBIA'S DEMOCRACY

"Tiyende pamodzi ndi mtima umodzi"
– Let's walk together in unity

Zambia has long been seen as a beacon of peace and stability on the African continent. This has largely been attributed to our first Republican President, Dr Kenneth David Buchizya Kaunda, who united the country after Zambia gained independence in 1964 under the national motto, "One Zambia, One Nation". Zambia is made up of over seventy ethnic groups, so unity was never a given. During his twenty-seven-year tenure in office, Kaunda would frequently burst into the refrain, "*Tiyende pamodzi ndi mtima umodzi*" which literally means, "Let's march together with one spirit". Zambians frequently intermarry between the different tribes and largely get along very well. This united spirit came under threat during the ten-year regime of the Patriotic Front Party which ruled from 2011 to 2021. Seeds of division and tribal and regional hatred were sown in a quest to rouse populist sentiments. During that time, Zambia embarked on a path of steep democratic and economic decline. Many watched in silent and fearful horror as our "proud and free" country became unrecognisable. Others, the brave few, stood up to the government's demagoguery to salvage our nation from the jaws of autocracy.

Zambia is a country in the heart of Southern Africa linked to its many neighbours by not only its borders, but also a rich history of solidarity at a time that was particularly risky for us to do so. Kenneth Kaunda, the father of our nation, instilled that legacy in us, but it really is something that is innately African – *ubuntu* – I am because we are. He used that ethos to support the liberation struggles of countries neighbouring Zambia such as Namibia, Angola, Mozambique, and even further afield, like South Africa. It meant that Zambia was a target of attacks by foreign countries targeting the resistance movements. This may in part explain Kaunda's decision to hold a successful national referendum in 1972 to turn the country from a multi-party democracy to a one-party state. In the economic boom years of the 1970s to the early eighties, Kaunda faced little internal resistance to his rule.

But our economic fortunes took a turn for the worse in the eighties. On 30th June 1990 there was a failed coup attempt[15] headed by Lt Luchembe Mwamba. Food riots ensued following the increasing cost of basic commodities in shops.[16] Under increasing political pressure, President Kaunda called for national elections under the new 1991 Constitution that reintroduced multi-party democracy in Zambia; a concession made in the face of the end of the called war and the continental shift towards multi-party democracy. Ultimately, Kaunda was unseated by the Movement for Multi-Party Democracy in 1991, whose presidential candidate won seventy-six per cent of the vote,[17] making Zambia one of the first African countries to change political parties peacefully through the ballot box. It's worth mentioning that Kaunda conceding defeat and stepping down peacefully has been monumentally responsible for the successive changes in power that Zambia has effected through the ballot box. For that, we owe him a huge debt. Almost all of Zambia's eight neighbours, and many countries well beyond our borders, are still being ruled by the political parties that were in power at the time of their independence.

The new President, Fredrick Titus Jacob Chiluba, was a very charismatic man who had a style of speaking that borrowed heavily from the evangelical church. He declared Zambia a "Christian nation" which was placed in the preamble of our Constitution. However, that did not stop his administration from being considered one of the most corrupt regimes in Zambia's history. Zambia's economic woes continued under his watch, but the economy was liberalised, foreign exchange controls were lifted, national assets were privatised.[18] This came with many casualties. Many employees of privatised state entities lost their jobs. This was also the peak of the HIV pandemic and at the time, life-saving drugs were very expensive and in short supply. Hundreds of thousands of Zambians lost their lives. However, Chiluba managed to survive his constitutionally mandated two terms in office which was due to end in 2001. In around 2000, some of his ministers began to suggest that Chiluba should seek a third term in office by amending the two-term limit in the Constitution.[19] Chiluba himself said very little on the subject, but as the calls for his third-term bid grew louder, a coalition of church leaders, civil society actors, trade unions, and the Law Association of Zambia banded together to prevent Chiluba from amending the Constitution. The Oasis Forum, as it became known, successfully lobbied the public to reject Chiluba's third-term bid.[20] Chiluba backed down, but not before anointing his successor, Levy Mwanawasa, who had previously stepped down from the position of Republican Vice-President in Chiluba's government, citing rampant corruption.

President Levy Mwanawasa was elected to office amidst allegations that his party, the Movement for Multi-Party Democracy, had rigged the election in his favour, defeating popular rival Anderson Mazoka of the United Party for National Development (UPND).[21] Mazoka declared himself the winner of the election and a presidential petition ensued,[22] which was only determined in Mwanawasa's favour towards the end of his first five-year term in office.[23] During his first term, Mwanawasa sought to prove himself by asserting his independence from his predecessor by waging a war against corruption. His primary target was President Chiluba himself, who was proving to be a threat to his presidency.

After protracted criminal prosecution, Chiluba was eventually acquitted of the charges against him in 2009.[24] The whole process had put a strain on his physical health and left him in the political wilderness. President Mwanawasa died in office after suffering a second stroke while attending an African Union Summit in Egypt on 29th June 2008.[25] In retrospect,

Mwanawasa is widely viewed as having been one of the best Presidents that Zambia has ever had, mostly due to the fact that the country's economic policies began to bear fruit during his tenure. He was succeeded by his Vice-President, Rupiah Banda, who defeated his nearest rival, Michael Sata, in a presidential by-election held in August 2008.[26]

President Rupiah Banda had been a career diplomat in the Kaunda regime before retiring when the MMD came into office in 1991. He was a jovial man known for enjoying the finer things in life. He came into office on the back of relative economic prosperity but was dogged by widespread allegations of personal extravagance which ultimately made him very unpopular amongst many Zambians. Veteran opposition Patriotic Front leader Michael Sata capitalised on this. In the run-up to the next general election in 2011, Sata promised Zambians that he would kick out Chinese investors and put "more money in your pockets".[27] During his election campaign, he urged them to accept whatever inducements they were given to vote for President Banda but instead vote for Sata's party, a strategy coined "*donchi kubeba*".[28] Sata won the election in a tight race[29] and was sworn into office on 23rd September 2011 as the fifth President of the Republic of Zambia.[30] Again, Zambia managed to change the guard through the ballot box.

Between 2011 and 2021, Zambia was on a path towards authoritarianism and democratic decline. That story is greatly intertwined with my own as that is when I entered the arena of what I call "legal politics". Sata's victory was widely celebrated by many Zambians who had rejected the opulence of the short-lived presidency of President Rupiah Banda. Not only had President Sata promised Zambians more money in their pockets, but he also promised to deliver a new constitution within ninety days.[31] This was meant to address some of the constitutional challenges that had long plagued our country, such as excessive executive authority and the lack of devolution of power. I have no doubt that President Sata had good intentions to lift Zambians out of poverty, but unfortunately his "Santa-economics" put the country on a path towards increasing debt and poverty, heightened greatly by his successor, President Edgar Lungu.

President Sata was a gruff man with the common touch and a sense of humour that greatly tickled his followers and offended the objects of his hilarity in equal measure, including the heads of states across the region. Much as human rights and the rule of law appeared to be a mild irritant, he did ultimately yield to professional legal advice. His untimely death on 28th October 2014, four days after our fiftieth Independence Day anniversary, plunged the nation into mourning and political uncertainty.[32]

Sata's Vice-President was a white man named Guy Scott. Although Scott had lived[33] in Zambia all his life, he did not qualify to become President in Zambia following an amendment to the Constitution that required a presidential candidate's parents to be "Zambian". This was a fallacy as, to date, all Zambian presidents have been born prior to Zambia's independence in 1964; so technically none of their parents were "Zambian". This is particularly so as prior to independence, Zambia, formerly called Northern Rhodesia, was part of a federation including Southern Rhodesia, now Zimbabwe, and Nyasaland, now Malawi. Nonetheless, the greater political "threat" in the minds of many Zambian politicians was to once more be ruled by a white person. Many Zambians of my parents' generation and above had vivid memories of life under an oppressive white minority colonial government. Patriotic Front members tried to depose Scott through political machinations[34] and Edgar Chagwa Lungu emerged as the "anointed" successor to Sata. It is unclear what attributes Sata saw in Lungu, but he presented himself as a humble man of the people.

Following a presidential by-election in January

2015[35] in which he narrowly beat his main contender, Hakainde Hichilema, Edgar Chagwa Lungu ascended to the office of President of the Republic of Zambia on 25th January 2015.[36] In Zambia, a presidential term in office is tied to the life of Parliament, which is dissolved every five years in readiness for the general elections. Subsequently, President Lungu's first term in office lasted one year and seven months. Soon, worrying signs began to appear.

The political tensions heightened in the pre-2016 general election period, leading to the outbreak of pockets of violence. Political skirmishes between the ruling Patriotic Front and the main opposition party UPND were growing and there were increased breaches of the rule of law. Parliament was dissolved in May 2016, three months before the general elections on 11th August 2016. Constitutionally all Ministers and Deputy Ministers were obliged to leave office after the dissolution of Parliament, as their position were dependent on being members of Parliament. LAZ sued every Minister, Deputy Minister, and Provincial Minister in their personal capacities for staying in office after the dissolution of Parliament contrary to the Republican Constitution. We eventually got a judgement in our favour in August 2016, but this is where the attacks on LAZ began. They were mainly directed at me as the President of

LAZ and were very vicious, aimed at discrediting me and the Association. No one thought that a Zambian court would rule in our favour over such a politically sensitive case. On the eve of the 2016 general elections, the Constitutional Court ruled in favour of LAZ, ordering every Minister and Deputy Minister to pay back all the emoluments that they had received after the dissolution of parliament.[37] This was a landmark victory for the Association. But this jubilation was short-lived.

The Zambian Constitution, which is the supreme law of the land by which all inhabitants of Zambia are bound, sets out the parameters within which the people of Zambia should be ruled. It provides for the separation of powers of the three arms of government: the Executive, the Legislature, and the Judiciary. It provides for checks and balances on these three arms of government. At the heart of constitutionalism and the rule of law are the judiciary. They are the guardians of constitutionalism and the rule of law in Zambia. It is subsequently imperative that we have a strong, independent, and impartial judiciary.

The judiciary has a duty to the people of Zambia to uphold the law regardless of the personalities or subject matter involved. Unfortunately, this has not always been the case. As the Law Association of Zambia said in 2012:[38]

> *"While we are strong proponents of judicial independence, we are equally stronger proponents of judicial accountability. Judicial independence and judicial accountability are not inconsistent and therefore can coexist. The judiciary should not be elitist or untouchable."*

Since the 2016 amendments to the Constitution, Zambia has seen a rise in lawfare: the fighting of political battles through the courts. Often such cases are determined in favour of the State or the ruling party. The Constitutional Court newly created by the 2016 constitutional amendments came under the spotlight as it was solely mandated to adjudicate over the presidential election petition that followed the 2016 general elections. Article 101 (5) of the Constitution requires that the presidential election petition must be heard within fourteen days of the filing of the petition. During the presidential election, petition controversy arose as the Constitutional Court reversed its decision to extend the time for hearing the petition over a weekend, leading to suspicion of extra-judicial interference. Also, controversy arose over whether the presidential petition had to be heard or determined within the fourteen days. Overall, the public was dissatisfied with the manner in which the proceedings took place and public confidence in the

Constitutional Court fell. In that case LAZ opted for a closed-door meeting with the judiciary over condemning them publicly.

In 2017, a case was brought in the Constitutional Court to determine whether the incumbent, President Edgar Lungu, had served two full terms in office as he had taken over the presidency following the demise of his predecessor. Under our Constitution, a President can only hold office twice. In November 2017, President Lungu threatened the Constitutional Court judges not to follow the Kenyan court example on the issue of whether or not he was eligible to stand in the 2021 presidential elections.[39] Also, during November 2017, the presidential press aide Amos Chanda gave an interview on the public broadcaster suggesting that any judgement against a Member of Parliament from the ruling party was not in the interests of justice. The statements went further to suggest that there would be repercussions against any judge that rules against a ruling party Member of Parliament. LAZ came out strongly to condemn the attacks on the judiciary. Nonetheless, the judgement came out in 2018 in favour of the incumbent, declaring that he had not served two full terms in office but stopping short of declaring him eligible to stand in the 2021 general elections.

LAZ continued to speak out strongly against

various breaches of the rule of law, political violence, and attacks against the judiciary. This in turn led to intensified attacks on me personally and LAZ generally by mainstream media that supported the government and on social media. In December 2016, a group of Patriotic Front cadres demonstrated in the city centre with professionally printed banners denouncing me and calling on me to step down. This was following a strong statement by LAZ condemning attacks on the independence of the judiciary by the presidential spokesperson. The Secretary-General of the Ruling Party declared me a "political enemy".[40] He even threatened to report me to my Chief for not aligning myself with their tribal agenda that sought to marginalise those who did not hail from the North or East of Zambia. Soon thereafter, three ruling party MPs held a press conference saying that if LAZ did not change, they would take steps to dissolve LAZ.[41]

CHAPTER FOUR:

IMPEACHMENT

"Sometimes people try to destroy you, precisely because they recognize your power – not because they don't see it, but because they see it and they don't want it to exist."

– **bell hooks**[42]

According to a 10th March 2017 article in *Slate:*[43]

"Of the 146 nations with data reported by the World Economic Forum in 2014 and 2016, just 56 have had at least one year with a woman as head of government or state over the past 50 years. Compared to men, these women didn't last long in office. In 31 of the 56 countries, women have been in the top role for five years or less, and in 10 of them, they only stayed one year. The average length

> *of tenure for the world's leaders of nations is far higher. On top of the 56 nations who've had at least one year of female leadership, there are 13 countries who've had women as heads of state or government for less than a year, usually as interim or acting leaders. Ecuador and Madagascar, for instance, each got the benefits of women as leaders for two days. Women are very likely to be brought in as interim leaders or likely-to-fail scapegoats after men have caused a scandal or otherwise mucked up. This is known in business and politics as the 'glass cliff'."*

Around the time that that article was published, it was my head on the chopping board. Not only were the positions of those on the LAZ Council under threat, mine included, but also, for the first time in its history, LAZ itself faced an existential crisis. I was resolved that the ship would not sink on my watch.

In December 2016, LAZ had decided to offer free legal assistance to a senior lawyer, Mr. Nchima Nchito SC, who was representing the owners of *The Post* newspaper in a legal action for its liquidation, purportedly on the grounds of tax evasion. Mr. Fred M'membe and his lawyers had been labelled by the ruling Patriotic Front government as being part of "The Cartel" aimed at bringing down the government. At the time, *The Post* newspaper was the largest and most influential private newspaper. Mr. Nchito had subsequently been slapped with the criminal charge of "impersonating" the Liquidator of *The Post*.[44] The LAZ Council, which I headed, decided that Mr. Nchito's independence as a legal practitioner was being infringed upon and subsequently asked Mr. Musa Mwenye SC to represent him in court on a pro bono basis. I was warned about the potential risks of taking such an action but I believed in the sanctity of the independence of the legal profession and so we proceeded accordingly.

The facts of the matter were that Mr. Nchito SC challenged the appointment of the Provisional Liquidator of *The Post* newspaper in the name of the shareholders of the company on the basis of the principle set out in the Supreme Court authority of *Avalon Motors Limited (in Receivership) v Bernard Leigh Gadsden & Motor City Limited*[45] which states that the directors or shareholders may challenge the appointment of a receiver in the name of the company. Both Mr. Nchito and *The Post* newspaper were viewed as enemies of the State. LAZ defended him because we believed that his independence as a legal practitioner was being infringed; according to Rule 22 of the Legal Practitioners' General Rules 2002,[46] every legal practitioner has a duty to act independently:

> *"A practitioner shall retain professional independence and ability to advise clients fearlessly and objectively and shall not permit the requirements of an introducer to undermine this independence."*

In response to LAZ's defence of Mr. Nchito, four busloads of ruling Patriotic Front cadres arrived at the LAZ Secretariat and demonstrated outside our offices, calling on me to come out publicly and form my own political party. Some were carrying weapons. During this period, ruling party cadres were widely feared. They consisted of violent political gangs that had taken over the operation of markets and bus stations, intimidating anyone who did not support the ruling party or wore the wrong political party colours. In self-defence, opposition political parties also had their own gangs of cadres. Luckily, on this occasion, no one was hurt as the Patriotic Front cadres failed to enter our offices. I called the police who quickly dispersed them. The demonstration was contrary to the Public Order Act, but no action was taken against them.

The Public Order Act is a law passed down to Zambia by her former colonisers that seeks to control public gatherings in the country. We have seen the Public Order Act used as a weapon against dissenting voices over many years. After that incident, all branding on LAZ premises and vehicles was removed to prevent our staff from becoming the target of political hooligans. During my two-year term, there were many periods when I feared for my personal safety. I used the drivers from LAZ to drive me around during office hours during this time. This meant that I had to restrict my trips to mainly official business. This also meant that I didn't have a social life to balance the stresses that I was experiencing. I spent many a sleepless night worrying about how things would end whilst trying to portray a façade of strength when on official duty. There were many days when I wished that I could cry to relieve the pain and tension that I was experiencing, but alas, no tears would come.

In April 2017, a ruling party Member of Parliament published a draft bill in the national press, threatening to repeal the statute under which LAZ is formed and to create multiple law societies in its place.[47] There were only around 1,000 lawyers in Zambia at the time and creating multiple societies would have weakened LAZ's voice. This was an unprecedented move; never in the history of our country had ruling party elites sought to abolish the Bar Association; not even during the authoritarian one-party state which ran from 1972 to 1991. Naturally, the LAZ membership was afraid of this threat, as was I, but as the head of the organisation, I had to be the calm in the storm. The LAZ Council got to work rallying the support of the membership and local and international partners. I remember older family members, who had friends in the legal profession, urging me to get the assistance of senior members of the Bar to help LAZ out of the predicament that we were in. I visited the offices of several State Counsel, who held the highest rank at the Bar, particularly those aligned with the government, asking them to use their influence to save LAZ. I was disappointed on almost every occasion. I came to realise that they were not prepared to put their heads above the parapet as they felt they had more to lose by appearing to challenge the government.

There were a few notable exceptions: Mr. John Sangwa SC, Mr. Musa Mwenye SC, Mr. Mutembo Nchito SC. But the greatest disappointment for me was the absence of the voices of young lawyers, who were in the majority in the legal profession. Even university students, who traditionally had held protests against previous oppressive regimes, were seemingly coopted by the government. Such was the level of fear, division, and oppression in the country. We had to use whatever political connections we had to the ruling party to lobby the government to neutralise the threat. A delegation from the SADC Lawyers Association and the International Commission of Jurists came to Zambia to meet the Minister of Justice and to offer solidarity. It was then that I really appreciated the old adage that a friend in need is a friend indeed. But ultimately, we were at the mercy of the government, who had a clear majority to pass the bill should it have been tabled before Parliament.

In March 2017, a group of ruling party-affiliated lawyers led by Patriotic Front stalwart Kelvin Bwalya Fube, or "KBF" as he was otherwise known, moved a motion for the impeachment of the LAZ Council on the grounds that we had deviated from our statutory mandate.[48] Under our Legal Practitioners Rules, once such a motion is moved, it must be heard. An extraordinary general meeting was convened to hear the motion. A few days before the EGM was scheduled to take place, the same group of ruling party-affiliated lawyers, led by lawyer KBF, filed a case in court to request that proxies be permitted by lawyers who could not attend the meeting physically.[49] This would have been a disaster as the lawyers had the full weight of the ruling party behind them and may have been able to collect a huge number of proxies in their favour. We accidentally discovered that this application had been made to court. A LAZ member had alerted us that the application had been filed in court. The LAZ Council was unaware of it as the court process had not come to our attention.

I subsequently went to the LAZ Secretariat and asked the Secretary who was temping with us if she had received the court documents. She promptly pulled out the documents, which had been under a pile of other documents. It turned out that the court hearing was the next day and we quickly retained Mr. John Sangwa SC as our Counsel. The young temporary Secretary, whom we had intended to retain, was quickly relieved of her duties. The following day we attended court and waited anxiously for the court to deliver its ruling that evening. The case was dismissed. I had never been more relieved about a court outcome. The next day would be the actual EGM.

On the eve of the EGM, KBF took to the airwaves to denounce me and the LAZ Council. He also alleged that I was on the payroll of the opposition UPND Party. I could not believe how confidently he could just make stuff up. I was also fearful that people would believe his lies and that the EGM would go against the LAZ Council. Not long before, he and his fellow plotters had organised a meeting at Chrismar Hotel, owned by a close friend of President Lungu, to rally LAZ members behind him. The EGM was scheduled for the morning of 29th April 2017. I got to the hotel bright and early and made sure to shake the hands of as many LAZ members as I could before the proceedings began. I was nervous, scared, even. I was determined to finish my term in office; the fate of future female LAZ Presidents could possibly have rested on this. As the proceedings went on, it became clear that the membership, however opposed to LAZ being "too political", were united about the fact that they did not want the government to interfere with how they run the Association. Before the motion was put up for a vote, one of the LAZ Council members came up to me and whispered in my ear that the movers of the motion wanted to withdraw it. I quickly seized the opportunity, and the movers of the motion withdrew it. The meeting was subsequently aborted. More relief!

The space for independent views in Zambia was shrinking. After *The Post* newspaper was shut down, several other media houses were threatened and attacked. Civil society was being stifled. The country was polarised along political and tribal lines which even divided the Church. In April 2017, the leader of the opposition, Hakainde Hichilema, was arrested on treason charges for failing to give way to the presidential motorcade,[50] which heightened political tensions in the country. The case was withdrawn several months later.[51]

In May 2017, the first President of LAZ, Mr. Africa Bruce Munyama SC, died. At his valedictory service, I used the occasion to not only celebrate his life, but to also affirm that LAZ would stand steadfast in its mission to uphold constitutionalism and the rule of law. Addressing a bench of Supreme Court Judges and people in the court gallery, I said the following:

> *"Today we bid farewell to a legal luminary named Africa Bruce Munyama. Our deepest condolences go out to his wife, Charity, and his three sons, Bruce, Keith, and Africa, and his six grandchildren. By all accounts, Mr. Munyama was a gentleman in the truest sense of the word. He was the son of a Methodist preacher, born in Southern Rhodesia in September 1938. Mr. Munyama was a brilliant yet unassuming man. He went to school at the highly celebrated Munali Boys Secondary school where he finished his school certificate. He later trained as a Barrister at the well-renowned Gray's Inn in the 1960s and was admitted to the Bar in 1963. He returned home afterwards in time to find and then marry his bride a week before Zambia attained its independence in 1964. He practiced at the Ministry of Legal Affairs before becoming the first indigenous Permanent Secretary at the Ministry of Legal*

Affairs, as it was then known, where he served the government until the late sixties. After he retired from government, he went back to practising law with his cousin, Mr. Edward Jack Shamwana, another distinguished and well-respected lawyer at the esteemed firm of Shamwana and Company. He was the nephew of another famous Zambian, freedom fighter and politician Harry Mwaanga Nkumbula, who supported him during his education…

But Mr. Munyama will always be remembered by LAZ as having been one of the architects that transformed the Law Society of Zambia into the Law Association of Zambia. The creation of LAZ was prompted by the need to create a body that embraced lawyers from both the private and the public sector; legal practitioners as well as judges. It also created a more Zambian identity at a time when lawyers were already being trained locally. He became the first President of LAZ in 1973, having been elected by an overwhelming majority. He was also the first indigenous Zambian in our history, pre- or post-independence, to head the Bar Association. So proud of his Association was he that he remained a paid-up member of LAZ right up until his untimely demise on 26th May 2017. As *the current President of LAZ, it is my honour and privilege to walk in his footsteps.*

This poem by Victorian poet Christina Rossetti best sums up what his greatest legacy will be:

"Not, How Did He Die, But How Did He Live?"
Not how did he die, but how did he live?
Not what did he gain, but what did he give?
These are the units to measure the worth
Of a man regardless of birth.

Not, what was his church, nor what was his creed?
But had he befriended those really in need?
Was he ever ready, with word of good cheer,
To bring back a smile, to banish a tear?
Not what did the sketch in the newspaper say,
But how many were sorry when he passed away.

Africa Bruce Munyama, we, the members of the Law Association of Zambia, are very sorry to see you go. Your work lives on in and through us. Long live the legacy of Africa Bruce Munyama, long live the Law Association of Zambia!"

Lawyers' valedictory sessions are always attended by the current Attorney-General or Solicitor-General, who are constitutionally mandated to be the legal representatives of the government. It was a defiant speech, intended to send a clear message to the government that LAZ had a long and rich history and that that legacy would continue.

Speaking the truth to power can be risky, particularly in countries where democracy is on the retreat. On 7th July 2017, I gave an address to the Pan-African Lawyers' Union. Seated next to me was Tundu Lissu, the President of the Tanganyika Law Society, the Tanzanian Bar Association. He had his own horror stories to tell of life under the authoritarian rule of President John Magufuli. After our session, we exchanged our respective presentations and joked that we would probably find ourselves in jail before the end of our terms in office. Exactly two months later, Mr. Lissu, who was also an opposition Member of Parliament in Tanzania, received sixteen gunshot wounds from unknown assailants in the parking lot of his parliamentary residence in Dodoma.[52] Luckily, though he was severely injured, he survived and had to go into exile in Europe for five and a half years following a failed national presidential bid.

There was a feeling by some members of LAZ that the Council of LAZ brought its troubles on itself by not engaging enough with government. Whilst it may be true that LAZ could have engaged more with government, it is also true that there was a reluctance on the part of the government to engage with us. The government took a "you're either with us or against us" stance which made operating as an independent organisation very difficult. I think that the events post the general elections, which include the short-lived declaration of a threatened state of emergency, an attempt to overhaul the Constitution to make it easier for the incumbent to remain in power, and rising legal authoritarianism, have vindicated us.

On 6th May 2017 LAZ held its annual general meeting. Our guest of honour was the Minister of Justice, Mr. Given Lubinda. In my speech at the LAZ ball, which I had written that evening in about ten minutes, I said this:

> *"...the Law Association of Zambia was formed in 1973 under the initiative of the then Attorney-General, Mr. Fitzpatrick Chuula, who as leader of the Bar sought to bring together all lawyers in the Association whether Barrister or Solicitor, or State Advocate or private practitioner under one umbrella under a set of common interests which we now refer to as Section 4 of the Legal Practitioners Act. This past year has seen LAZ go through some of the most challenging trials in its history. We are now at a time where society is extremely polarised, and LAZ has been a victim of this scourge. But following the events of the last couple of weeks, it is gratifying to see that we are again speaking with one voice*

as a stronger and more united Association. As a Christian living in a Christian nation, I cannot go without saying to God be the glory. He is indeed the Way, the Truth and the Light and of that fact I am here to bear testimony…

Honourable Minister, for me by far the greatest takeaway for me and other members of the Association is that the last few weeks have shown that indeed the legal profession is united and resolute in pursuing its mandate for the benefits of its members and the society we serve. We have indeed affirmed that united we stand, divided we fall. And we have chosen the path of unity. I have lamented that the polarisation that we see in society according to tribe and political affiliation. As His Excellency President Edgar Lungu said in his 17th March address to Parliament:[53]

'We are all alive to the fact that Zambia is made up of seventy-three ethnic groupings. This is a fact that we cannot hide, change, or ignore. National unity is an essential pre-requisite for the development of our nation. Despite our divergent ethnic, social, religious, and political backgrounds, we have a shared heritage and destiny as a country, which oblige us to co-exist in unity.'

If nothing else, I think that the LAZ is a shining example of the fact that all divisions and differences of opinion can be resolved through dialogue, and we at LAZ are more than willing to lead the way in fostering dialogue even at a national level if and when called upon to do so.

Lastly, Honourable Minister, after a very challenging period, we breathe a collective sigh of relief that we are on the path towards building a stronger LAZ by introspecting on the ways that we as an Association may perhaps also have to reform ourselves in order to be more effective in executing our mandate over forty years after our founding statutes were enacted. As Nelson Mandela once said, 'After climbing a great hill, one only finds that there are many more hills to climb.' But for now, we pause to relax and celebrate what has been a challenging yet successful year, and may we raise a toast to several more to come."

I had lived to fight another day. The LAZ AGM and the two-day law conference that had preceded it had gone by in a blur. I had sensed the hostility of the LAZ membership at having caused so much turmoil and upheaval in the Association.

I remember the first time that I realised that I had lost the support of the LAZ membership. LAZ had hosted what we called mentorship circles for our junior lawyers, something that I had initiated in the Association under our mentorship programme, just before my final AGM as LAZ President. The mentorship programme had originally started out as one-on-one relationships between mentors and mentees, but it soon became apparent that many lawyers were either too busy to commit the time or lacked the necessary chemistry to take the relationship forward. The mentorship circles were organised so that there were three keynote speakers on three different topics. The junior lawyers would sit at a table of ten consisting of two mentors, one male and one female, and eight junior lawyers. After the three facilitators had given their presentations, the mentees would engage with the mentors at their table on the topics and then rotate after fifteen-minute intervals so that all the mentees would interface with as many mentors as possible. It was a bit like speed dating.

As the host, I gave the opening remarks and there was an awkward silence – nobody clapped. Once the discussions began at the tables, it became clear that none of the mentees wanted to be at my table. For the entire duration of the event, only four or five mentees visited our table, opting instead to overcrowd the other mentors' tables. It dawned on me that I had spent so much time trying to survive my term, keep safe, and deal with the onslaught of political battles that the LAZ membership did not really know who I was or what I stood for outside of what they mighy have seen on television or heard on the radio. I surmised that, with little other information to work with, they had filled in the gaps with the rumour and innuendo that had surrounded me.

My last days in office were very painful, made worse by the fact that my successor, who had been elected unopposed three weeks before the conference, had effectively rendered me a lame duck president for the remainder of my term in office. The rest of my term was no less challenging, but I did make it to the end.

It was a tradition that in a LAZ election year, the outgoing President would give their final speech and then hand over the mantle to the incoming President, who would then give their inaugural speech. The highlight of the gala dinner was the fact that I had managed to persuade former South African Public Protector and rock star Thuli Madonsela to be our guest of honour. She was someone I had looked up to and admired on my journey to becoming LAZ President. She had been in office for seven long years, enduring several slights and a lot of political pressure in holding the South African government to account. I considered her to be a kindred spirit. I regarded it a huge privilege that she had come at all, but more especially because she had travelled to Zambia soon after the death of legendary South

African anti-apartheid activist Winnie Madikizela-Mandela. She wore a black *duku* on her head as a sign of mourning. Thuli Madonsela was as lovely in person as I had imagined, soft-spoken and calm. She was to give the keynote address at the LAZ gala dinner after my speech.

The speech I gave was meant to be a call to those in the new LAZ Council to exercise courage and do the right thing, even when it was not expedient. I acknowledged the fact that, while I was the first female LAZ President, I would not and should not be the last:

> *"I have been working within the Association for close to ten years. I am passionate about everything it stands for: justice, honour, and integrity. I love my siblings, but they are always sure to humble you no matter how lofty your position. On our way to the airport a couple of weeks ago, I told my brother that I would miss serving on the Council of the Association as it had almost become a part of who I am. His response: 'You know you don't own LAZ, right?'*
>
> *Indeed, much as I love working for the Association, all good things must come to an end. I had hoped that by stepping down I would be setting an example for Presidents all around the world,*

and particularly in Africa, that there is life after the presidency and that there is no shortage of good leadership to take your place, but President Ian Khama of Botswana beat me to it!

Over the last few days, the world has been commemorating the lives and work of three giants in history: Dr Martin Luther King, Jr; Dr Maya Angelou; and Mama Winnie Madikizela-Mandela. As a civil society activist, all of them have had a profound influence in my life. In line with the theme of our conference, 'Power, Privilege and the Pursuit of Justice', I recently read the book Khwezi by Redi Tlhabi. So compelling was the book that I read it from cover to cover in a few hours. It is the story of former South African President Jacob Zuma's rape accuser and how she was vilified, humiliated, and eventually exiled for daring to speak her truth to power. In much the same way, I have watched the world trying to tame Mama Winnie in death. I know why the caged bird sings.

Too often the powerful and the privileged try to diminish the voice of women by bullying them into silence. This is not something that is unfamiliar to me nor indeed many, many women including our amazing guest of honour. We will not be silenced. Women belong in positions of leadership and influence. We deserve to be anything we want to be, even presidents. I hope that when the next woman President of LAZ comes, and there will definitely be another woman, she will know that it is her competence, her intelligence and her intrinsic worth as a human being that makes her deserving of the position. I hope that in my own way that I have shown that women can perform at the highest levels of any organisation no matter how challenging the role.

Tonight, we are privileged to have Professor Thuli Madonsela as our guest of honour. As the former Public Protector of South Africa, she rose to prominence by challenging the abuse of state power and resources in extremely challenging circumstances. In the words of the title of her biography, she is 'No Longer Whispering to Power'. Indeed, more of us need to clear our voices and use our privilege to express our concern over matters that affect our country. We may feel far removed from events that happen in our country, but it is all of our problems, and we must all work to improve the lives of our fellow citizens in whatever way we can. As Martin Luther King, Jr. once said, 'An individual has not started living until he can rise above the narrow confines of his individualistic concerns to the broadest concerns of all humanity.'

I would like to end my speech by expressing

my thank yous. Thank you to the members of the Association for your support and for entrusting me with this position. We went through some challenging times, but we pulled together and rode the storm, as one. Thank you to the members of the outgoing Council. Your commitment and hard work were commendable, and I am exceedingly proud of what we have achieved together. Thank you to all the Secretariat staff so ably led by our dependable Executive Director, Mr. Edward Sakala, for all your hard work. Thank you to our friends in civil society, professional bodies, the public, and the media who provided feedback and support to the Association in various ways. Thank you to all those whom I relied upon for advice. Thank you to my friends and my campaign team who made it possible for me to even be here.

I would also like to thank my family for their unwavering support. My mother, Dorothy; my sister, Mubanga; and my brother, Mutale have been rock-solid in providing love, comfort, and support during my tenure.

Finally, to the incoming President Eddie Mwitwa, who is very worthy of this position, and the incoming Council, I would like to echo the words of Professor Madonsela: 'Throughout my life, I have learned that the most important critic whose

> *judgement of my actions matters, is my conscience'. I wish you all the best and I have every confidence that you will lead the Association to new and greater heights!"*

The atmosphere in the audience was tense. People clapped politely as I ended my speech, but no one had laughed at my attempt at a joke at the beginning of my speech. Thuli Madonsela gave her speech after mine, also acknowledging the passing of Winnie Madikizela-Mandela. It was now time for my successor, who had previously been my Vice-President, to give his speech. He began his speech by pronouncing an end to "politicking and fame-seeking". I felt like I had been slapped in the face by the person who had been right by my side through all the hardships that I had endured during the course of my two-year tenure, now realising precisely what he thought of me. I stood up to shake his hand at the end of his speech according to custom. As soon as the formalities were over and the dance floor was opened, I left our new President to bask in the glory of his new-found "fame".

I had spent much of my term championing gender diversity in leadership and in the profession. Much to my dismay, the Council that I had led which had seen the highest number of women elected, possibly ever, was replaced by a largely male-dominated Council. According to the *Slate* article referenced earlier:

> *"Most of the world's female heads of state and government were replaced by men, and most countries who've had a woman at the top have only ever had one. It's been said that a country's second top female leader is the true harbinger of progress in gender equity, because the failings and qualities of the first are often ascribed to her gender."*[54]

Was this to be my legacy? I'm happy to report that the current LAZ Council, elected in 2022, has a very healthy representation of women and I believe we may soon see another female LAZ President.

CHAPTER FIVE:

POWER AND VULNERABILITY

"It's easier to run for office
than it is to run the office."
– Thomas P. O'Neill, 47th Speaker of the United States House of Representatives

We often hear leaders on the public stage being urged to "have a thick skin". I have read many autobiographies of world leaders and recognise in them the hurt that they were not allowed to show in a bid to portray the façade of strength. In the current digital age in particular, public figures have to deal with more personal attacks than ever before and it does take a toll on you. My term at LAZ ended in May 2018. I felt hurt at the rejection by the Association to which I had devoted seven years of my life. My body, which for the last two years had been in a constant state of hypervigilance, was broken. I succumbed to a very nasty flu which lasted a good three weeks. I had been given three weeks off by my law firm and returned to work thereafter.

I had worked for the same law firm for fourteen years by that point but following my experiences at LAZ, I no longer felt like I fit in. So much had happened in the last two years, and I was no longer the same person. I felt like I needed another break, so I applied for the Draper Hills Fellowship at Stanford University. I got in and went away for a period of three weeks from July to August 2018.

If my experience on the Fellowship taught me nothing else, it taught me that I needed to heal. I was physically and emotionally burnt out from my harrowing experiences during my tenure at LAZ. This manifested in fatigue, irritability, anger, and even depression. The World Health Organization[55] has recognised burnout as "a syndrome conceptualised as resulting from chronic workplace stress that has not been successfully managed. It is characterised by three dimensions: feelings of energy depletion or exhaustion; increased mental distance from one's job, or feelings of negativism or cynicism related to one's job; and reduced professional efficacy." Bolstered by adrenaline, I had powered through the previous two years without much time to rest or to grieve the loss of my child. When I did feel the pain of the many pressures and indignities that I had had to endure, I was unable to cry. This was not because I was insensitive to the pain; on the contrary, the pain was so great that it was numbing.

Former US President Ronald Reagan once said, "if you're explaining you're losing". Just as in politics, it can be difficult to explain the events that happen in your life in the moment. This may be because the truth is nuanced and context specific. I am a great admirer of Hillary Clinton and supported her bid for the presidency in 2016. In my view, her greatest weakness was the fact that she lacked the likeability factor. She has a serious demeanour and lacks charisma, unlike her husband, former US President Bill Clinton. But perhaps just as damaging, Hillary Clinton, on the campaign trail, liked to explain her policies in great detail. Her opponent, Donald Trump, on the other hand, was the king of the soundbite and short on elaborating on how he would achieve his campaign promises. It made Trump's message easier to sell.

Like Hillary Clinton, I'm not the most likeable character – I'm serious, introverted, and opinionated. As a result, it's often assumed that I am a snob and have an inflated opinion of myself. If that was the case before I became burnt out, becoming burnt out alienated those around me even further. I often joke that being the founder of an organisation means that you automatically become the "Chief Everything Officer". By that I mean that in all departments, be it human resources, programming, finance, monitoring and evaluation, or administration, the buck stops with you to ensure that you maintain the values and standards of the organisation; in line with my personal values of honesty, integrity, and excellence.

We started Chapter One Foundation with just five employees, three of us being lawyers. Because we filled in a gap in civil society by providing a legal perspective on human rights and governance work, our services together with those of LCK Chambers were in demand. We were expected to be at several different CSO workshops and events *and* manage our own workload. Only two of the lawyers were experienced, which meant that as well as everything else I had to train the third. Running a civil society organisation was completely new to me, I relied heavily on the experience of our programmes officer Josiah Kalala, who had previously worked in donor aid organisation. He was the systems and processes guy; I was the vision carrier. I often felt completely out of my depth and overwhelmed, as did some of our staff as this was a learning curve for all of us.

Eventually we built up institutional capacity by putting in place a strategic plan and policies to guide us. About a year in, Josiah came to see me in my office. He told me that he had obtained a scholarship to do his Masters in the UK and would subsequently do a fellowship in the US. This meant that he would be away for a whole two years. On the one hand, I was delighted for him, he is extremely bright, talented, and deserving, on the other hand, my heart sank – what would I do without him?

I gave Josiah two years' unpaid leave. He was a very valuable member of the Chapter One Foundation team, and we didn't want to lose him. He left in September 2020, less than a year before the national general elections. The environment in Zambia was becoming increasingly polarised due to the tribal and political agenda of the Patriotic Front. Josiah's absence was greatly felt, not only had he provided guidance on systems and programmatic areas; he had also helped shoulder the burden of leading the organisation.

We did hire a programmes officer to fill in for him and eventually added more staff but most of them lacked the requisite level of experience. As time went on, the pressures began to mount. There was more work to do, and with the elections drawing near, there was the increasing threat of our organisation being targeted for our working in protecting the rule of law and human rights defenders in an ever more authoritarian environment. We took on high profile cases such as the case in which we challenged the eligibility of the incumbent President, Edgar Lungu, to stand in the 2021 general elections. Everyone in the country was becoming increasingly more fearful, including our staff.

We had done security training and installed a security system in our office but that didn't seem to help. When I asked the lawyers on our staff to write articles for publication in the press on rule of law and governance issues, none of them were even prepared to put their names in the byline. This indicated to me that perhaps they were not yet ready for frontline activism. So, as I did when I was President of the Law Association of Zambia, I put my head above the parapet on behalf of the organisation.

I felt that the growing threats to the country and our organisation called for me to lead from the front, the stakes were high. In retrospect, I should have reflected more on the fact that this had not proved to be a winning strategy at LAZ. On the contrary, I was accused of trying to hog the limelight and to "make a name for myself", a view held by many to this day. This was laughable to me because I knew the great personal cost of doing so, rightly or wrongly, both times I had felt that it was the right thing to do in the circumstances. It's not that I wasn't afraid, I was very afraid, I just didn't feel that I had many options.

I spent many a fitful night wondering how the situation in the country would end and what would become of me if things did not go well. Meanwhile, not only was I facing an external threat, but the strain of holding it together while running the organisation was beginning to take its toll. I am one of many short-tempered people in my family, but for all my life, including my time at LAZ, I had managed to refrain from any major public outbursts. I had become run down, fatigued, and irritable, not only with my staff, but also with my colleagues in civil society whose expectations of us began to overwhelm me. The national elections in August 2021 came and went, thankfully ushing in the winds of change and bringing a return to a state of political stability.

By December 2021, I told the Chapter One Foundation Board that I was struggling and needed a sabbatical. The problem was that there was no one in the office sufficiently senior or experienced to hand over to; Josiah would only be back in June 2022. This had added to the pressure on me because even when I took a "break" from work, there was no leaving work behind, I was always "on". This was an introvert's nightmare. I gradually became more withdrawn at the office, preferring to work from home in a bid to conserve my energy. I observed that this withdrawal was misunderstood by my staff as being a form of laziness, but I didn't know quite how to explain that I was burnt out.

Matters came to a head in April 2022. I had booked a "week off" with my mum at a health spa in South Africa to try and regain some strength. In the days before I was set to leave there was an incident at the office. I felt that one of my staff members had spoken out of turn and so I arranged a meeting with the team to explain the virtues of team unity and the appropriate channels of communication. The incident had upset me, but I had planned to hold the meeting more than twenty-four hours after the event, giving me sufficient time to calm myself and collect my thoughts – I even had a written script of what I was going to say. What happened at that team meeting became a big source of regret.

The team was assembled in the meeting room awaiting my arrival. I came in and left the door open, sat down, and began my presentation. I didn't go very far before I was interrupted by the very subject of our meeting. It was like someone lit a match in a gas-filled room – pouf! I completely lost it. I was so angry that my entire body was shaking with rage. My script was abandoned, and I began a tirade about the need for team unity, the fact that we were a feminist organisation and subsequently we shouldn't try and bring other women down. Regrettably, amongst other ominous statements, I also told the team not to "shit where they eat" and said it twice for good measure. When I was done the team were in stunned silence. I picked up my things and somehow managed to walk to my car still trembling with emotion, banged my car door, and drove off. In the fallout from that meeting, two members of my team resigned.

Anyone who knows me well will tell you that swearing at people is very uncharacteristic of me, especially not in the workplace where it is completely unacceptable – even if provoked. This was a clear case over the response totally negating the provocation. My real friends will also tell you that I am not a vengeful person. *Mea culpa.* I truly regret it, not least because it became fodder for those for whom I was already viewed as an arrogant, self-absorbed, and even selfish. Aside from my very small circle of friends, no one has outrightly confronted me about this incident, which was widely circulated, preferring instead to use innuendo, metaphor, and conjecture. Worse still are those people who I have known for years who chose not to raise the issue with me at all but began to treat me differently. I have now been labelled every negative female trope from a queen bee to the B word. What hurt me most, however, was the allegation that I bully the young ladies under my charge. For most of my career, I have really tried to promote and protect the interests of women as much as I could. I am no saint, but neither am I a bully. Unfortunately, there is no way of dispelling these impressions of me because they fit nicely into the stereotype of the mean female boss.

A few days after my outburst, I went to the health spa in South Africa to decompress and gather myself. I was away for a week, I felt a little bit rested afterwards, but as anyone who has suffered burnout will tell you that is insufficient time to recover. I got back to the office to a scared and resentful team. I addressed them over the incident twice, even apologising, but the damage had been done. All that was left for me to do was to hang on until Josiah got back in June 2022 so that I could take a much needed four-month sabbatical.

In March 2022, I was nominated by a donor agency to do a fellowship in Budapest, the capital of Hungary. I accepted the nomination because I figured that it might be good to get away for a while and because the fellowship was in a subject that I was very interested in, constitutional law. I was accepted onto the course and about three weeks before I was due to travel, I began to doubt whether

I was in any shape to travel. This was a month before "the great outburst". I wrote to the course facilitators asking if it was possible to defer my entrance to the following year. They replied that my place was not guaranteed if I deferred. I was the only Zambian on the course; if I didn't travel, there would be no Zambian representative and an opportunity would be lost. I conferred with my family and friends who all encouraged me to go. Josiah returned at the beginning of June 2022. It was quite a relief. I couldn't start my sabbatical immediately as we were winding up our audit. The course started at the end of June 2022, and I decided that I would travel after all.

Aside from the fact that I wasn't in good health, I had some trepidation about travelling to Budapest. Hungary was being led by Prime Minister Viktor Orbán, a dictator of note whose government has clamped down on freedom of expression, and undermined plural democracy and judicial independence, and has taken an anti-immigrant stance. However, when we got there, I did not experience any negative sentiments from the locals, apart from the one taxi driver that overcharged me. The university in which the fellowship was hosted had a good reputation in the field of constitutional law. However, my time in Budapest was far from pleasant. My withdrawal from social engagements and group activities was misunderstood by my fellow participants as snobbery and arrogance. But worst of all I didn't have the mental capacity to complete the course readings and therefore had to try my best to wing it. I withdrew from the course two days before completion, unable to withstand the negative impressions I had made on the participants and staff. I just wanted to go home to people who loved and understood me.

If you have ever known political persecution for advancing the cause of democracy, the rule of law, and human rights, then you will know what a lonely and tiring journey it is. My friend Thulani Maseko knew how it felt. He had spent almost one-and-a-half years serving a jail sentence as a prisoner of conscience, living in deplorable conditions at His Majesty King Mswati's pleasure. His crime? Criticising the administration of justice in Eswatini or Swaziland, as he preferred to call it. He was released from jail following massive local and international pressure on the Swazi authorities to release him. Like his hero Nelson Mandela, Thulani left jail more resolute to champion human rights and democracy, not only in Swaziland but also across the region. Thulani was assassinated by unknown assailants on the evening of 21st January 2023 as he was watching television with his family.[56]

In 2017, I was the beneficiary of Thulani's

benevolence. Then, I was the President of the Law Association of Zambia. At the time, the Patriotic Front had only been in office for a couple of years but were still very popular amongst the masses. The government had begun to demonstrate an intolerance for human rights and the rule of law in Zambia, taking us down a path that surely would have led to the end of true democracy in Zambia. Because so many Zambians were in support of the government, it became costly to speak out against the excesses of the government. Those of us who dared to do so were labelled as "anti-government" and worse still, "unpatriotic". We were subjected to smear campaigns in the media and threats of violence from ruling party supporters. Matters came to a head when members of the ruling party threatened to dissolve the Law Association of Zambia.

During that time, there was a lot of silence from those that I had previously considered friends. Many were too afraid to publicly show their support for fear of losing favour with the government or suffering reprisal. Many believed that we had brought these troubles on ourselves, preferring to keep their heads down to avoid the blows of political forces undoubtedly more powerful than themselves.

Around April 2017, LAZ received word that a delegation from the International Commission of Jurists, then led by Arnold Tsunga, and the

SADC Lawyers Association would be coming to offer solidarity to LAZ and to meet the Zambian government to dissuade them from abolishing LAZ. Thulani Maseko was in that delegation. Words cannot express the sense of relief and comfort that Thulani and the rest of the delegation provided; we were not alone after all.

That was not Thulani's last mission to Zambia. He came as a trial monitor under the auspices of the Southern African Human Rights Defenders Network when Zambian activists Laura Miti and the late Bornwell Mwewa were prosecuted on frivolous charges.[57] Thulani was an all-weather friend to many.

Thulani was a kind, gentle, but brave soul. In his own words at the Oslo Freedom Forum, "we shall never surrender, for we know there is a price to pay for the truth."[58] His death will not be in vain. For me, his legacy is one of tireless advocacy for the defence of human rights, the rule of law, and democracy. He embodied the words of Martin Luther King Jr. by offering solidarity wherever injustice reared its ugly head. This really was another manifestation of something inherently African, *ubuntu* – I am because we are.

For me, Thulani's death was a stark and sad reminder to everyone that there are many people in the region and in the world facing political persecution who need our help, and we must offer it. Here, I pause to remember the murders of Rwandan journalist John Williams Ntwali and Cameroonian journalist Martinez Zogo in the early part of 2023. But many more still live amongst us. For example, I can think of my sister Martha Chizuma, who is facing political persecution for upholding the rule of law and trying to stamp out corruption in her native Malawi. And the perennially prosecuted Zimbabwean lawyer and politician Job Sikhala. We must not forget what Thulani stood for: no retreat, no surrender.

Being a leader and having influence often involves taking face-saving measures, in order to give the appearance of strength. The pressure of trying to appear flawless or even infallible is huge and exhausting. Being in a leadership role comes with power and influence, but what is not often talked about is how emotionally vulnerable leaders are. This is particularly true in Africa, where many people are afraid of admitting that they are sick, tired, or scared as all these are seen as a sign of weakness. The higher they rise, potentially, the longer the fall, and that creates a lot of insecurity. As a friend and fellow leader pointed out to me, very few leaders feel comfortable opening up about the personal challenges of leadership. So few of us are prepared to accept our human frailty. We often say that we are okay when we are not.

The advent of various social media platforms has created additional pressure to be seen to be happy and successful. I had a conversation with other leaders about just how ugly things can get behind the scenes. Faced with my own struggles with vulnerability, I reached out to other leaders whom I know in the African Diaspora, and asked them three questions:

- What does power (inner strength and external influence) mean to them?
- What does it mean to be vulnerable?
- And when do they allow themselves to be vulnerable?

Without exception, in one way or another, everyone I asked said that power was having control and vulnerability was losing it.

A friend of mine, "Paul", confessed to me that he was struggling. He was a very successful businessperson earning millions of South African Rands per year, and one day, that was all gone. He had to sell four properties and his luxury car in order to pay his employees' salaries. He told me that he knows four executives that had committed suicide this past year alone over personal struggles. He grew up poor and knows all too well what it means to have no money, a place he felt confident he would never return to again, and yet he finds himself anxiously facing that possibility once more.

Another friend of mine, "Angela", was a successful international journalist who returned to her home country in Africa to make a difference. The toxic political environment in her country overwhelmed her, and she had to re-evaluate how to use her writing skills for the good of her own community, make ends meet, and take care of her extended family.

Both Paul and Angela told me that although they were struggling, they had relied on their Christian faith. They trusted that all would be well despite their prevailing circumstances. They talked about authenticity being the essence of vulnerability. Stripped of everything that once defined them, they now have a new outlook on life. Paul now wants his legacy to be that when he dies, people will tell his children how kind and considerate he was. Angela's true identity is as a communicator who bridges the societal divisions, a sister, daughter, and a Christian.

In her book *The Gifts of Imperfection*, vulnerability research expert Dr Brené Brown said that she has found that, "Perfectionism is not the same thing as striving to be your best. Perfectionism is the belief that if we live perfect, look perfect, and act perfect, we can minimize or avoid the pain of blame, judgement, and shame. It's a shield. It's a twenty-ton shield that we lug around thinking it will protect us when, in fact, it's the thing that's really preventing us from flight."[59]

Robert G. Ingersoll, describing US President Abraham Lincoln, once said, "Nearly all men can stand adversity, but if you want to test a man's character, give him power."[60] For me, power – however illusory – means having options and having control over them. For me vulnerability means not being able to determine my future. When do I allow myself to be vulnerable? When I go to the gym barefaced. For the rest of the time, my makeup hides the battle scars of standing up for what I believe in, of being an introvert in a very public space, and of being told who and what I am by people only interested in headlines. And yet as leaders, we put ourselves out there because we want to be seen, we want to be heard, and we also want to be counted. As Angela says, our contradictions are who we are. Leaders are encouraged to have a thick skin, but even "thick-skinned" people have a soul.

Being vulnerable requires character. As Helen Keller was quoted as saying, "Character cannot be developed in ease and quiet. Only through trial and suffering can the soul be strengthened, ambition inspired, and success achieved."

Brené Brown suggests that rather than ask "What have I accomplished?" we should ask ourselves, "How can I improve?"[61] That is a lot less pressure on us.

Too often too many of us think that if we allow ourselves to be vulnerable, we will lose our power. I am not advocating telling all your secrets to all and sundry. In fact, Brené Brown advises that people should earn the right for you to show them your vulnerabilities.[62] No one, no matter how powerful, is infallible or invincible. As a powerful woman, I have to redefine what success means to me outside of my status or position, barefaced in front of a mirror, powerful, yet vulnerable, and authentically me.

CHAPTER SIX:

BATTLING GOLIATH

"The very thing that makes
the giant so terrifying is also
the source of his weakness."

– Malcolm Gladwell, *David and Goliath: Underdogs, Misfits, and the Art of Battling Giants*[63]

When I got back from my fellowship at Stanford in August 2018, I applied for a six-month unpaid sabbatical from my law firm. I needed space to think. Never one for being idle, I continued to work in civil society in the background, deliberating over national issues, and drafting joint civil society statements. It became clearer to me that I could not go back to working at my law firm. I felt that there was still more work to be done to stem the tide of our declining democracy. As my six-month sabbatical came to an end, I became more resolved. I went back to work in

April 2019 and by May I had put in my resignation.

Before the end of my sabbatical, I had travelled to Johannesburg to meet up with the Amnesty International colleagues led by Deprose Muchena whom I had met through my work at LAZ. They encouraged me to create an NGO that would fill the gap in civil society for legal defence and advocacy. There I was introduced to Roselyn Hanzi, the Executive Director of Zimbabwe Lawyers for Human Rights (ZLHR), an organisation that I had long admired for the excellent work they do in Zimbabwe in defending human rights and the rule of law. Rose kindly arranged for me to travel to Zimbabwe for a study tour of ZLHR in Harare. Whilst there I met the staff and some of the Board members and was taken through their operations. I was very impressed by the size of their operations and the orderliness of it all.

In April 2019, I was elected Vice-President for Africa of the Commonwealth Lawyers' Association.[64] I had arranged for the biennial Commonwealth Lawyers Conference to be held in Livingstone, Zambia that year, the first time it had ever been held in Zambia. Once again, I experienced the fickle nature of "politics" as there was much fanfare made by the press and lawyers about my election. During the conference I met up with Arnold Tsunga, whom

I had met through training and workshops in the region. He further encouraged me to set up an NGO like ZLHR, which he had been the Executive Director of for several years. By this point I was sold. But I was also broke after the two-year sabbatical that I had taken to become LAZ President, and the further six months unpaid leave that I had taken. I had earlier written a draft grant proposal with support from the Amnesty International office in Joburg. I approached the Swedish Embassy for funding after presenting them with the proposal. They agreed to fund the initiative but would only do so indirectly through one of their facilitating partners.

I met up with the grants manager at the organisation that I had been referred to by the Swedish Embassy, under which Chapter One Foundation obtained a sub-grant. As it happened, the week that we signed the sub-grant agreement was his final week in office. He put us on a six-month "pilot programme" and promised us that he had "ring-fenced" funds for us should the pilot project be successful. The funds became available in May 2019, and on 8th July 2019 we were open for business.

Chapter One Foundation is named after Chapter One of the Laws of Zambia which contains the Constitution. The Constitution is the supreme law by which every Zambian, regardless of status, is bound.

As qualified lawyers, we take an oath to uphold and defend the Constitution, and we at Chapter One take that oath very seriously. I simultaneously set up a law firm called LCK Chambers which is currently the only law firm set up as a social enterprise in Zambia. LCK Chambers does Chapter One's legal work pro bono and in addition takes up some commercial work as a sustainability effort to support the work of Chapter One Foundation.

People thought I was crazy to leave my law firm in order to set up Chapter One Foundation, an NGO. Maybe I was, but I did so because I believed I was called to serve in the area of protecting human rights and the rule of law in Zambia. It is definitely one of the hardest things that I have done, but as the philosopher Friedrich Nietzsche said, "He who has a why to live for can bear almost any how."[65]

As I was scrolling through LinkedIn one day, I came across a post by Womba Silumbu-Kankondo, another lawyer who had recently quit her job. She said that like me, people thought she was crazy to quit her cushy job at a bank in order to set up her own practice. She loved her job and her colleagues, but she explains her decision to quit like this:

> *"[A] time came, as does for everyone, when I knew I needed to spread my love to more people. To share*

> *my gift with the world unlimited by time and space. For almost seven years, I was a servant of one master. But my calling is much bigger, I was called to be [the] servant of many masters. I only needed to listen to the still voice [within] to learn…this. Where was I to start from? From the beginning. Firstly, by providing a service that people needed and was useful. Secondly, I was going to live by the 'law of mutual exchange.' And it therefore follows that as I have contributed to prosperity…I have in turn prospered – riches untold!"*

This was my story. I embarked on my new path at a time when it was very costly to do so. The work that we went on to do involved speaking truth to power and defending those who might otherwise not have had legal representation. The alternative was to remain silent and to keep one's head down to avoid the blows of a force undoubtably greater than any individual. But what is the cost of silence? As Archbishop Desmond Tutu once said, "If you are neutral in situations of injustice, you have chosen the side of the oppressor."[66]

I believe that we are all called to serve in some shape or form. Paulo Coelho, author of *The Alchemist*,[67] urges us all to pursue our "personal legend": that thing that we were brought on earth to do – our purpose. US writer and politician Wes Moore says that in order to find our purpose, we must find our greatest joy that coincides with the world's greatest need.[68] As a Christian, I believe that whatever pursuit that might be, the underlying objective must be to try to serve with love. God bless those who are able to do this consistently!

Running an NGO is not easy by any means. We had a small staff and I had to oversee everything; I became the "Chief Everything Officer". But the staff were dedicated, and we began to make small gains. Our six-month "pilot project" was due to end in November 2019. About a month before it was due to end, I began to ask our sub-grantor when we could expect more long-term funding. We had hit all our milestones and they were happy with our performance at our end-of-project review. After being given the run-around for a couple of weeks, they finally got back to us to tell us that there was no more funding for us. We still had some funds remaining so they told us that the best they could do was to extend the project for a further two months, but that would not include funding for salaries.

To add insult to injury, our sub-grantor had disallowed about US$5,000 worth of expenses that we had used to furnish, partition, paint, decorate, and set up our office, which I had thought were covered under our budget line for furniture. I had to pay back within one week. This was money which I did not have at the time but had to find. Two of our Board members – Father Cleophas Lungu, then our Board Chairperson, and Sarah Longwe – and I went to see the Executive Director of our sub-grantor to see if there was anything more that could be done. She literally laughed in our faces, saying that that is why she could never set up an NGO. I was almost in tears. I had thoughts of moving back to my parents' house and selling everything I owned to keep Chapter One Foundation afloat.

Once I was done feeling sorry for myself, I set to work trying to find the funding to keep the organisation alive. I was desperate. I borrowed money from close family members to pay the salaries. I went round to about four law firms that I thought were friendly, pitching the idea of doing their debt collection for them. They gave me audience but none of them signed on. I was on my own. I myself did not draw a salary from November 2019 to April 2020. I did not tell the staff of our predicament at that time. In retrospect, perhaps I should have, but I feared it would only add to the pressure that I was under. I had also made a call to a colleague at the National Endowment for Democracy, whom I had engaged with whilst at LAZ, to see if they could help. They decided to give us funding, which came through in

April 2020. Also in April 2020, the payment of my equity share in my previous law firm came through. I was then able to pay off all our debts.

The COVID-19 pandemic was just beginning. Not only did I have to keep the organisation afloat, but I also had to do my best to keep my staff alive. We instituted very strict COVID-prevention protocols which included hybrid working hours, stringent sanitation procedures, and avoiding public gatherings – which unfortunately included restrictions on funeral gatherings. When I look back on this period, I remember God's grace. He has come through for me on many occasions and this would not be the last.

In mid-2019, the Patriotic Front Party, which had a large majority in Parliament, began to make moves to make substantial amendments to the Constitution[69] in a bid to entrench their hold on power. The Constitutional Amendment Bill No. 10 of 2019, or Bill 10, as it became known, became the biggest threat to Zambian democracy since the creation of a one-party state through Zambia's 1972 Constitution. It proposed amongst other things removing the constitutional limit on the number of Members of Parliament, making it easier to dismiss judges and to remove the Speaker of Parliament, and allowing the leading candidate in a presidential election to co-opt another political party to meet the

50+1 threshold to win a presidential election.

The tabling of Bill 10 followed political tension in the country that had arisen following the contested victory by the Patriotic Front government in August 2016. The leading opposition political party, the United Party for National Development (UPND) took out a presidential election petition which was thrown out on a technicality after the Constitutional Court controversially reversed its decision to allow the UPND leaders' lawyers to present their case beyond the initial fourteen days provided for. Matters came to a head when UPND leader Hakainde Hichilema was charged with treason for failing to give way to the presidential motorcade.[70] A threatened state of emergency was declared after a fire broke out at the largest market in Lusaka. To ease tensions, the Catholic Church and later the Commonwealth Secretariat tried to facilitate talks between the government and the opposition political parties. The government rejected these efforts on the basis that there was need to indigenise the dialogue. This became the pretext under which the government enacted the National Dialogue (Constitution, Electoral Process, Public Order and Political Parties) Act.[71] The stated objectives of the Act were:

(a) facilitate the implementation of the
Siavonga resolutions of political parties

relating to constitutional and institutional reforms, separation of powers and judicial independence, tolerance, freedom of assembly, and civility in politics and electoral reforms;

(b) provide for a national dialogue process to facilitate the Constitution refinement process and regulation of political parties, public order, and electoral process reforms;

(c) establish the National Dialogue Forum and provide for its functions; and

(d) provide for matters connected with, or incidental to, the foregoing.

The National Dialogue Forum was largely constituted of ruling party members of Parliament and civil society organisations friendly to the government. The Forum was to deliberate for ten days, which was later extended by a few days. Proceedings were closed to the public; in fact, it was a criminal offence to publicly reveal what had been discussed in the Forum. The two weeks of deliberation resulted in a draft electoral process bill, political parties bill, and draft constitutional amendments which would become known as the Constitutional Amendment Bill No. 10 of 2019.

Faced with an existential crisis, Zambian citizens and civil society organisations instituted a campaign against the runaway corruption in Zambia, as well as to reclaim citizens' right to effective participation in the country's democracy. The campaign also raised concerns about bad governance in the country with particular focus on the threat that the Constitutional Amendment Bill (Bill 10 of 2019) posed. The campaign, which was christened the "Yellow Card Campaign,"[72] was carried out largely via social media under the hashtags #YellowCard and #HandsOffOurConstitution. As in the game of football, the yellow card symbolised a warning to the government that they may soon be ousted from office for poor performance. A peaceful Yellow Card protest against corruption and bad governance was also held on Saturday 20th July 2019 outside the Parliament buildings. The #YellowCard campaign had a massive response from a general public who evidently had become very worried about the state of the nation with #YellowCard holding the record for a hashtag on Zambian Twitter.

Chapter One Foundation played a prominent role in the fight against Bill 10. LAZ had taken out a petition in the Constitutional Court to challenge the constitutionality of decisions and procedures that had led up to the Bill being tabled in Parliament. We had initially approached LAZ's lawyers about LCK Chambers being co-counsel on the case but when they proceeded without us, we decided to take out our own petition making slightly different arguments. The drafting of our petition was largely done by Chapter One Foundation's Josiah, a studious and diligent member of our team. We successfully applied for the two petitions to be consolidated under one case, which meant that they would be heard side by side. The arguments we made were very nuanced and difficult for many people, even lawyers, to grasp. On the first day of trial, I noticed that the gallery was empty. This was one of the most important cases of our time and no one appeared interested in it. So, I decided to call attention to it whilst balancing my ethical duty as a lawyer not to tout our law firm. I posted this on my Facebook page:

> *"Calling on all Zambians!*
> *Dear All,*
> *As you know, LAZ and Chapter One Foundation took out a petition to challenge Bill No. 10. Trial began on 12th November 2019. I have been greatly saddened by the lack of interest by the public, CSOs, and especially fellow lawyers. This is probably the most important case in the history of Zambia after Harry Mwaanga Nkumbula tried to stop Zambia changing into a one-party state in 1972. The stakes are just as high in this case and yet the court gallery is empty.*

I am calling on all Zambians to show solidarity to demonstrate how important an issue this is. The next trial date is on Wednesday 20th November 2019 at 09:00 hours. It's likely to be the last day of trial. Please show your solidarity!"

My Facebook post was carried widely on social media and in the press.[73] The next day, the court gallery was full of journalists and ordinary citizens who came to follow the proceedings. The gallery remained full for the rest of the case and the case was widely reported. However, ultimately the Constitutional Court dismissed the case in a judgement that I believe misconstrued our arguments. After the judgement was delivered, both the LAZ President, Eddie Mwitwa, and I spoke to the media and urged Members of Parliament not to pass the Bill. I said, "We respect the outcome of the judgement. The judges have spoken, but it's still incumbent on the citizenry to ensure that Bill No. 10 does not pass because it will be very detrimental to our democracy and to our rights and freedoms as citizens of this country. [Citizens] can speak to their MPs; they can show their displeasure on social media and by any other legal means."[74] I tried to take a photo of both our legal team and the opposing legal team after the judgement was pronounced but understandably no one was interested. Zambia had lost. We then redirected our efforts towards advocating for the Bill to be defeated. We had lost the battle, but the war was just beginning.

The only positive thing that came out of the Bill 10 petition was the fact that Zambians were now very much aware of what was at stake. Civil society organisations went all out to de-campaign Bill 10 on radio and on television programmes and I too participated in such programmes. We shared out the various programmes between us. On 2nd December 2019, I appeared on a television programme with the LAZ President, Eddie Mwitwa, to discuss the ramifications of Bill 10. It went very well; it was a live call-in programme. I had prepared for it and was on top of the material. When I got back home that evening, I received a call from Hot FM requesting me to come on their breakfast show the following day to discuss Bill 10. I was under the impression that I would be the only guest on the programme. I agreed to attend as none of the other civil society members were available and besides, I had just been on television discussing the same topic; what could go wrong?

I arrived at the studio on time, with my notes. A few minutes later in walked Tutwa Ngulube, Patriotic Front Party Member of Parliament for Kabwe Central and Deputy Chief Whip. I was surprised to see him there but unfazed. But when the programme began, it was clear that I was no match for Tutwa's political machinations. Tutwa appeared to be referring to information that I did not possess, and I floundered. I did my best to maintain my composure, but the damage had been done. It appeared that I was defending the indefensible and people began to doubt whether there was anything bad about Bill 10 at all. I had failed in my task. To add to my humiliation, Hot FM decided to play the recording repeatedly to demonstrate that "the great" Linda Kasonde was not all that smart after all. I tried my best to defend myself against the barrage of online criticism of my radio performance, but in retrospect, I should have allowed the incident to pass without comment. I hadn't performed well; that was a fact. It was a bitter pill to swallow.

With my credibility damaged and my confidence having taken a knock, it took a lot for me to get back on to a radio or television programme to talk about Bill 10 again. But I had to remain mission-focused; Bill 10 was bigger than all of us. We all did our part; the Laura Miti-led Alliance for Community Action conducted an amazing social media campaign informing people of the evils of Bill 10 using simple language and infographics that everyone could understand. They also published the telephone numbers of all the Members of Parliament, urging citizens to call them to express their displeasure with Bill 10. This had never been done before. Many ordinary Zambians did not even know it was possible to make requests of their Members of Parliament. Through the advocacy of civil society actors and the opposition, the government failed to meet the two-thirds majority required to pass Bill 10 – not once but twice. This was despite rumours of attempts by the government to bribe Members of Parliament and propaganda to promote the Bill. The opposition political parties led by UPND also played a major role in Bill 10's defeat. With the exception of three UPND Members of Parliament, they had all walked out of the parliamentary chamber at the time the vote was tabled, leaving the Patriotic Front Members of Parliament unable to convene a coram to pass the vote.[75] When it became clear that the government's final attempt to pass Bill 10 before the 2021 general election had failed, Laura Miti called me, and we both screamed in delight, not quite believing the feat we had all managed to achieve. It was one of the happiest days of my life!

There were two other big challenges that came the way of Chapter One Foundation. In the run-up to the August 2021 general elections, the incumbent, Republican President Edgar Chagwa Lungu, had made it clear that he would stand for re-election. Chapter One Foundation supported the view that President Lungu's bid for re-election was unconstitutional as he had previously been elected to office twice and it would therefore constitute an unconstitutional third term. After President Lungu filed his nomination papers, John Sangwa SC approached us to add our name as a litigant to the petition challenging Lungu's eligibility to stand for a third term.[76] This was another moment of fear and trepidation for me. It appeared that the Lungu government would stop at nothing to get re-elected. Nonetheless, we signed up for the fight, as did Sishuwa Sishuwa.

As on previous occasions, I had sleepless nights contemplating what might happen to those of us standing in the way of the Patriotic Front's return to power. During the trial, mobs of Patriotic Front cadres surrounded the courtroom. This made it a no-go area for me. But on the day that the judgement was being delivered, I decided that I would go to the Constitutional Court to witness the proceedings. I got dressed, wearing a pair of trainers with my suit, ready to run if the need arose. I took a taxi to court for fear that my car might be recognised. I sat through as the court delivered its judgement, ultimately disappointed that the judges dismissed our case.[77] Outside court, journalists were waiting for a comment from me. I told them that the Court had spoken and that we respected its decision and the ball now lay in the court of the electorate. I urged Zambian citizens to come out and vote.

Polling day was scheduled for 12th August 2021. Throngs of people turned out to vote in the cold of the Zambian winter in unprecedented numbers, some queuing up the night before. Zambia was one of a handful of countries to hold a general election during the COVID-19 pandemic. Nothing could stop citizens from casting their vote, so much was at stake. Our freedom and the state of our economy were on the ballot. Graduates showed up wearing their graduation gowns, a symbol of protest at the lack of employment opportunities. There was jubilation when the first set of voters came out of the polling station; the mood was buoyant. I got to the polling station before five a.m. and was in the queue for three or four hours. At around midday, all social media platforms had been shut down to try to stifle the movement of information about the election results. Luckily, Chapter One Foundation had anticipated this. We had drafted pleadings in advance, preparing ourselves for a challenge in the Constitutional Court.

On the day, however, we had to change tack because history had taught us that the Constitutional

Court would not give us a constitutional injunction ordering the government to restore the social media platforms. I redrafted the court application for judicial review in the High Court where it was more likely that we would obtain a court order to restore all internet services pending a full hearing of the case. I filed the papers on the afternoon of 12th August 2021. By evening, we had received the court order restoring the internet services.[78] This court order was by no means a foregone conclusion; at the time we obtained the order, it was unclear which way the election was going. Judge Charles Zulu had bravely put his neck on the line.

Now that we had the order, we had to serve it on the Zambia Information Communications and Technology Authority, better known by its acronym, ZICTA, the government body that controlled the gateway for all internet services. That wasn't easy; their office was shut, which meant that I had to find an employee of the Authority to serve it on. Using the contacts I had, I managed to trace one of the employees. My partner and I drove through the night to deliver the documents to their house. It was around 9 pm and eerily quiet as people were at home waiting for the election results. It bears mentioning that, in an unprecedented move, the government had deployed the army on the country's streets to maintain order, so we didn't know what to expect. Finally, after taking a few wrong turns, we arrived at the house and delivered the documents. By midday the next day, social media platforms were largely restored. It was a huge victory for Chapter One Foundation, and we received a lot of affirmation from ordinary citizens.

However, there was some disappointment, and even anger, in the legal fraternity because Chapter One Foundation had entered into a consent judgement with ZICTA which was carefully worded to avoid outrightly assigning the blame to ZICTA for the internet shutdown. Some lawyers wanted us to find out who was directly responsible for the shutdown and hold them accountable. We had not done so because we realised that ZICTA is a public institution. If liability for the shutdown had been assigned to them, they would potentially have been held liable for all the financial loss suffered by any Zambian who had been affected by the internet shutdown. We did not think that this was in the best interests of the taxpayers who ultimately would have had to foot the bill. Thankfully, when the election results were finally announced, the former President was voted out of office by a margin of one million votes and Zambia is once again on the path towards restoring our democratic values.

Since the movement to restore multi-party democracy in the late 1980s to early 1990s, Zambia has a rich history of opposing and resisting authoritarian rule. Zambians did so because we dared to imagine a different future. More importantly, the foundation of our success was premised on the initial success of the restoration of multi-party democracy after Kenneth Kaunda, a very powerful President both locally and internationally, magnanimously stepped down after being defeated in the 1991 general elections. This in turn led to the resistance of President Chiluba's bid for a third term in office, and Bill 10, not to mention several successful attempts to unseat regimes that were inimical to our progress as a nation. Beating insurmountable odds is as old a tale as the battle of David and Goliath. In his book, *Born a Crime*, Trevor Noah writes, "We tell people to follow their dreams, but you can only dream of what you can imagine."[79] As David Brooks once said, God would not allow you to imagine what you cannot achieve.[80]

CHAPTER SEVEN

FRIENDLY FIRE

"Do what you feel in your heart to be right – for you'll be criticised anyway. You'll be damned if you do, and damned if you don't."

– Eleanor Roosevelt[81]

The term "friendly fire" is an oxymoron that refers to firing ammunition at someone on your team or an ally on the battlefront. In 2020, I was once again thrust into the spotlight for pursuing a course of action that I believed was the right thing to do for the country. The amendments to the Zambian constitution in January 2016 necessitated the amendment or repeal and replacement of several statutes. Among these statutes was the creation of the Electoral Process Act enacted on 6th June 2016. Through that statute, the concept of continuous voter registration was introduced for the first time in Zambia.

Around 12th June 2020, the Chief Electoral Officer of the Electoral Commission of Zambia, Mr. Patrick Nshindano, held a press briefing at which he stated that the period for voter registration relating to the 2021 General Elections had been reduced to thirty days. The original period for voter registration was scheduled to be between 28th October 2020 and 30th November 2020. Towards the end of 2019, the government had also commenced a mobile registration process for national registration cards. National registration cards are the official national identification cards that every citizen must obtain at the age of sixteen. Green national registration cards are held by Zambian citizens and pink ones by foreign nationals who are permanent residents. The green national registration card is the only mandatory form of identification for voting. Reports were coming through that the registration process for national registration cards was being concentrated in the strongholds of the ruling Patriotic Front Party. This posed a danger that the election result would be unfairly tilted in favour of the ruling party. On 3rd August 2020, Chapter One Foundation filed a petition in the Constitutional Court arguing that the thirty-day limit on voter registration and the on-going national registration card registration process infringed on the constitutional right to vote.[82]

About a month later, I got a call from Musa Mwenye SC informing me that he had filed an application for judicial review in the High Court on behalf of some youth activists, including the celebrated activist and musician Pilato. Around that time the leading opposition party, the UPND, also decided to file an application for judicial review in the High Court challenging the decisions of the Electoral Commission. Also in September 2020, we decided to amend our petition to ask the Court to declare that "the geographical limitation to the issuance of national registration cards will result in the disenfranchisement of many Zambians in contravention of the National Values and is, therefore, unconstitutional." This happened to be one of the issues that the parties to both judicial review cases were challenging. The two sets of parties had come together and had been told by their respective courts that their cases could not proceed until ours in the Constitutional Court, which is a superior court, was disposed of.

Some time towards the end of the year, I had called for a meeting with the lawyers in both cases to see if there was some middle ground. They did not want to join our case and we did not want to abandon ours. Not long afterwards, a relative of mine who was a UPND supporter called me about the case. She told me that a very important person would be calling me to speak about the case. A day or two later, I got a call from the UPND leader himself, Mr. Hakainde Hichilema. He has a very deep and authoritative voice. We had a very cordial discussion about the case. He asked if Chapter One Foundation would withdraw its case, and I politely declined. The call ended and I thought that was that; however, friendly fire was about to be unleashed from an unexpected direction.

Zambian academic and respected historian Dr. Sishuwa Sishuwa used to publish an annual list of which public figures had impressed and which ones had disappointed him. On 27th January 2021, I made the top of his list of public figures who had disappointed. I was surprised to have made the list at all; our work at Chapter One Foundation had been meaningful and impactful, and only the previous year I was on the list of those who he thought had impressed. It felt like an unwarranted and unfair attack. He argued that:[83]

> *"The decision by the Electoral Commission of Zambia (ECZ) to discard a valid and lawfully established voters' register, numbering 6 million voters, and drawn up an entirely new one within a 30-day window could have been stopped if*

> *Linda Kasonde, the Executive Director of Chapter One Foundation, had not challenged it in the Constitutional Court in October 2020. Earlier in August, Kasonde had dragged the government to the Concourt seeking two reliefs: an order mandating the electoral body to carry out continuous voter registration and another directing the Ministry of Home Affairs to implement the mobile issuance of national registration cards throughout the country. In early October, she amended her petition to ask for a third relief: that the decision by the ECZ to 'disallow currently registered voters from voting in the 2021 general election is unconstitutional and therefor null and void'. In approaching the Concourt on this specific matter, Kasonde messed up big time and demonstrated poor judgement…"*

Sishuwa cited several reasons for my alleged lack of judgement. He said that I had refused to collaborate with the other parties who had brought cases in the High Court and had "held the whole country hostage" by not stepping aside to let other, more experienced lawyers pursue their cases. He argued that the Constitutional Court was not the appropriate venue for arguing the case given the fact that in its brief history, the court had a record of "frustrating time-bound and politically sensitive matters." "Argh", he lamented, "who advises Linda Kasonde. As a result of her intransigence, the historic opportunity to secure interim reliefs and arrest the faulty process initiated by ECZ was squandered or lost. Wittingly or unwittingly, she has participated in a plot to circumvent the electoral process and create a possibly dodgy voters' roll that is guaranteed to deliver a positive result for Lungu, the incumbent."[84]

It was a scathing attack from someone who, ideally, should have been an ally in the fight against the Patriotic Front's attempts to hijack democracy in Zambia. I had previously considered him to be a personal friend, and this felt like a betrayal. I felt he could have made his point without impugning my competence. I spoke to the Board of Chapter One Foundation about whether to respond to the article and it was decided that we should, as it was quite damaging. The response that we crafted[85] pointed out that in fact Chapter One Foundation had been the first organisation to take the matter to court and that we had been the first to reach out to the other parties to try to collaborate. We noted that the Constitutional Court, as a court of first and final instance, might have been the quickest way of litigating the issues at play, as opposed to the High Court, which potentially had another two layers of appeal, the Court of Appeal, and the Supreme Court.

In any event, injunctive relief even in the High Court was not guaranteed, especially in matters of a political nature. We stated that with twenty years of experience as a lawyer, I was hardly a novice. As my second boss was fond of saying, "There are many ways to skin a cat"; meaning that there was no one right way of approaching the case and the other parties by no means had a monopoly on wisdom either.

In retrospect, I could also have added that we weren't working on our own. We had decided to work with the Coalition of Christian Churches Monitoring Group, which was the largest election monitoring body in Zambia, and Governance, Electoral, Advocacy, Research and Service Delivery or GEARS Initiative, both being the leading independent authorities on elections in Zambia, as our witnesses. I felt that we had tried to defend ourselves as much as we could, bearing in mind that the case was still active in court and subsequently, we were unable to explain the intricacies of the case as our Zambian courts have strict rules against discussing active cases in the public domain.

What I was unprepared for was the tirade that followed in a series of articles by Sishuwa over the next few days under the screaming headline, "I Like and Respect Linda Kasonde, but She Messed up Big Time".[86] At that point I knew that it was not worth arguing. This was a good instance in which the old Bemba adage *tondolo musuma,* which means silence is golden, definitely applied. In the midst of these scathing attacks, my cousin Chileshe called to console me. He told me that no matter what the outcome, he was sure that I believed I had taken the right course of action, and I loved him for it.

As it turned out, despite the short timeframe for registering to vote, a record number of eligible voters had managed to register. On 25th February 2021, the Electoral Commission issued a press statement indicating that its Provisional Register showed that 7,002,393 voters had registered. The voter turnout on polling day, 12th August 2021, was equally unprecedented and the opposition ruling party won by a historic one-million-vote margin.[87] I was elated! Zambians had once again proved that their vote counted, and that impunity would not be tolerated.

Our case was finally scheduled for trial in August 2021, a few days after polling day. There is no telling whether the judicial review cases filed in the High Court would have met the same fate. Ultimately, we decided that we would withdraw the case as we feared that our case might be used as grounds to challenge the electoral results. On 16th February 2022, I gathered a group of likeminded NGOs that included Chapter One Foundation,

Alliance for Community Action, Young Women in Action, Centre for Trade Policy and Development, NGOCC, PAGAAZ, ActionAid, Zambia Council for Social Development, Council of Christian Churches in Zambia, Transparency International, GEARS, and Bloggers of Zambia and together we wrote a letter to the Chief Electoral Officer of the Electoral Commission enquiring as to whether there had been a policy shift on the issue of continuous voter registration in Zambia. We issued an accompanying press release to inform the public of our action.[88]

The Electoral Commission did not respond to us directly, but on 18th February 2022, they announced that they had scheduled engagement meetings with stakeholders, including civil society organisations, to discuss amongst other things continuous voter registration.[89] The meeting was held on 25th February 2022. By 1st June 2022, continuous voter registration was being implemented. There was no fanfare on the occasion celebrating the victory by civil society, but there was an editorial by the newspaper *News Diggers* on that day commending civil society organisations for helping make continuous voter registration a reality.[90]

I would like to speak about the cost of silence. There are definitely times when silence is golden, but too often it is used by people to make others shrink from taking up challenges and saying what needs to be said. During the Patriotic Front government's years in office, many Zambians were reduced to being fearful and cowed into submission at the thought of speaking truth to power. There's an old Japanese saying, "The nail that sticks out will be hammered down." Like Japan, Zambia is a high-respect culture that values conformity. This has served our people well in some respects, keeping family and community ties close, but it has also come at a price.

Years ago, I wrote an article in which I posed the question, "Is African Culture Killing Our Race?"[91] It was a response to a conversation with a highly intelligent African woman who had expressed the view that any differences that citizens may have with the leaders of African countries should be resolved quietly and privately to avoid exposing your country and our race to public and international ridicule. I doubt that these thoughts cross the minds of Western dissidents who challenge their own leaders. I believe that often, politicians only respond to criticism, positive or otherwise, when there is an audience that may affect their popularity – after all, politics is about numbers. Quiet diplomacy or appeasement is often ineffective unless that person has some actual influence over the erring individual. I consider it our solemn civic duty to point out when the "emperor" is walking around naked.

As a result of the massive levels of corruption witnessed under the previous Patriotic Front regime, Zambia has once again become heavily indebted to both local and international creditors. I am no economist, but I have yet to hear of any credible alternative to Zambia's current International Monetary Fund (IMF) deal given the impact of geopolitics on countries in the Global South. I do, however, want to talk about what led us to this point.

On 17th May 2017 six activists – Laura Miti, Bornwell Mwewa, Lewis Mwape, Sean Tembo, and Mika Mwambazi – gathered at Parliament to protest the procurement of forty-two fire trucks at the exorbitant cost of US$42 million. They were arrested and prosecuted for over a year for their efforts before ultimately being acquitted. When the few individuals and members of civil society spoke up against the rampant corruption and breakdown of the rule of law in Zambia over the previous seven to ten years, those people were labelled unpatriotic fearmongers. Very few people were willing to speak up against the excesses of the former government because it led to ostracization, humiliation, and demonisation.

But what about the cost of the majority remaining silent? In my view any austerity measures that Zambians may have to face as a result of the IMF programme are the direct cost of the silence of the majority when it mattered. Indeed, we must reflect on the fact that some lawyers were complicit in the plunder of our national resources. This must be a lesson to all of us that it is our civic duty to speak up and stand up and be counted when we see the signs of corruption and impunity. There is no such thing as a perfect government; however, we must always be faithful patriots. As journalist Paul Craig Roberts has been quoted as saying, "A true patriot does not confuse government with country. A patriot's loyalty is to his country, and loyalty to country requires holding government accountable."

When I was LAZ President, my uncle came to see me. He told me that he thought that I should stop speaking out against the government because I "would get crushed". I understood him very well. He had been an active participant in the movement for multi-party democracy in the late 1980s to early 1990s that would eventually unseat President Kenneth Kaunda and end almost twenty years of one-party rule. He warned me that nothing would come of my resistance to the government and even if it did, I would not receive any benefit from whatever government replaced them. I listened but did not contradict him. I knew that what I was fighting for was a worthy cause and the only thing that I really wanted from it was to put Zambia back on a democratic path. That would benefit everyone, including me.

The existence of democracy is underpinned by freedom of expression, assembly, and association. These rights afford citizens the freedom to hold opinions without interference and to receive and impart information and ideas through any medium. Ultimately, democracy depends on the participation of each and every one of us. If the last five to ten years taught us anything, it is that activism between elections is just as important as participation in elections. We must continue to remember that, or once again face the risk of losing the democratic ideals that we as a people hold dear.

Post the 2021 general election, I began to notice that an increasing number of young people identify themselves as "activists" or "human rights lawyers". Many of these people were not willing to put their heads above the parapet when the chips were down, afraid of being attacked or humiliated by the previous government. I have heard young lawyers ask how they can avoid the pitfalls that come with real activism. In my opinion, you can't insulate yourself from failure. Doing this work requires taking some risks, and there will be times that you miscalculate the potential repercussions, or you cannot avoid them. As Trevor Noah once wrote, "We spend so much time being afraid of failure, afraid of rejection. But regret is the thing we should fear most. Failure is an answer. Rejection is an answer. Regret is an eternal question you will never have the answer to. 'What if…' 'If only…' 'I wonder what would have…' You will never, never know, and it will haunt you for the rest of your days."[92]

The work that civil society does is often unglamourous, humiliating, and thankless. The wins can be very gratifying, and the blows can be very bruising. As an activist, one must always bear in mind the Solomonic words of Winston Churchill, "If you're going through hell, keep going."

CHAPTER EIGHT:

WOMEN, RESILIENCE, AND THE WILL TO LEAD

"Throughout my career, I had to bear the burden of being the only woman, the first woman. It's not something to celebrate. It's a serious commentary on a society that has not leveraged the talent of women."[93]

– Dr Mamphela Ramphele, anti-apartheid activist

With a woman's ambition to lead comes the risk of being undermined, maligned, sidelined, or even physically attacked simply because women are still viewed as the weaker sex. Having been elected as the first female President of LAZ, I now concur with the person who jokingly once said, "Don't be the first, be the second." On a serious note, being a relatively young female leader in a patriarchal society is fraught with challenges, the first of which is actually getting into office.

I had made deliberate steps towards becoming the President of LAZ over a period of seven years. During that time, I had been a keen student of leadership and politics. I knew for example that, in this cyber age, women leaders are often perceived as being less competent, less likable, and are far more likely to be the subject of verbal abuse on social media than men are. I was no exception.

Many women do not assume leadership roles because they do not think they are good enough. As mentioned earlier, Sheryl Sandberg pointed out that men will put their hand up to do a job that a woman with twice the ability will hesitate over. It is true that risking failure can have devastating and sometimes very public consequences, but what about the potential rewards of trying? There were two other male candidates for the position of LAZ President during the election and I beat them both on an issue-based campaign and without having to "bribe" a single voter.

Having taken a few positions contrary to the government line soon after I was elected, I was quickly perceived as being a member of the opposition. Bear in mind that two years earlier, just after having been elected Vice-President, the Executive of LAZ had been labelled by the press as being pro-government. However, as a leader irrespective of your gender, always remember one thing: "Don't believe the hype, it's a sequel." Those of you who are my contemporaries may recall that line from an eighties rap song by Public Enemy, which was very aptly named. It is another way of reminding us that Palm Sunday came a week before the crucifixion. We live in a world where false humility, particularly for women, is praised and genuine self-confidence is denigrated; where being average is viewed as a virtue and being ambitious, even for selfless purposes, is seen as a vice. Simply put, you will never please everybody, so do not go into leadership because you want to be popular. Regardless of whether the work is paid or voluntary, leadership is a privilege and should always be about service. If you want to be liked all the time, you are likely to be extremely ineffective and/or compromise your beliefs or values.

Both at LAZ and at Chapter One Foundation, our mandate is to promote and protect the rule of law, constitutionalism, good governance, and social justice as well as to regulate the profession. Whilst there are many things that we do outside our role as watchdogs on governance and rule of law issues, those are the issues that attract the most public attention. Often it means coming into conflict with the government. If, like me, you are unfortunate enough to be in office during a national election period, it requires taking a few calculated risks and a little audacity. Taking risks requires courage, and having courage makes the difference between achieving greatness and losing hope.

In January 2016, the Zambian Government made substantial amendments to our Constitution, including the provisions on how and when a Minister has to vacate office. The Government took the view that, following the amendments, the new position of the law was that the Ministers could stay in office even after the dissolution of Parliament. LAZ took the considered view that, even under the amended Constitution, it was still a requirement for Ministers to be Members of Parliament to qualify to hold the office of a Minister and to remain in office. Subsequently, when Parliament was dissolved, the Ministers were required to vacate their offices as had always been the position. LAZ took the matter to the newly created Constitutional Court to determine the matter conclusively.

As the President of the Association, I was not hugely popular with the government and was vilified in the media. We stood our ground and just a few days before the general elections, the Constitutional

Court pronounced a judgement in our favour, not only affirming that the Ministers should have vacated office upon the dissolution of Parliament, but in addition ordering that the former Ministers pay back their salary and emoluments for the period that they had illegally held office. It was a huge landmark decision. The point I am trying to make is that leadership comes with many challenges. Doing it right and for the right reasons is not for the faint-hearted. Sometimes you do need to be an "Iron Lady".

Another thing I would say to women who seem to be averse to looking a little foolish is this: do not be afraid of failure. As Denzel Washington put it in his 2011 commencement speech at the University of Pennsylvania,[94] "fail forward" with the faith that you can get up, dust yourself off and keep going. A few years ago, I came across a great article in *The New York Times* about US Supreme Court Justice Ruth Bader Ginsburg.[95] At the time she entered law school in the autumn of 1956, women made up less than three per cent of the legal profession in America. She got married and had two children whilst pursuing her graduate and post-graduate university degrees. As you can imagine, it must have been extremely difficult for her to reach the positions that she achieved having lived through times when sexism and sexual harassment were commonplace and even accepted.

At the time of the article, Justice Ginsburg was eighty-three years old and said she applied one piece of advice that her mother-in-law gave to her when she was getting married to almost everything she does, "In every good marriage, it helps to be a little deaf."[96] And when trouble comes, and it will inevitably come, using the recently deceased US Supreme Court Justice Antonin Scalia's favourite expression, she says, "Get over it!" Easier said than done as there are parts of your leadership journey when you will have to walk alone; standing firm with the belt of truth buckled around your waist and with the breastplate of righteousness in place, as the Good Book tells us. During that time, you must be the calm in the storm. Zambian wordsmith Chanda Mfula once wrote in a Facebook post that, "Character isn't built across the entire race, but during that extra mile you discovered you must run just when you thought the race was over."

It would be remiss of me not to mention that I would not have achieved the level of success that I have without the support and encouragement of many male friends and colleagues. Because of them I have risen up to become the first female elevated to being named partner in a top-ranked law firm. I think that my success at the law firm greatly helped increase my profile in the Law Association. The truth of the matter is we cannot empower women as leaders without male champions. But as former US Secretary of State Madeleine Albright once said, "There's plenty of room in the world for mediocre men, but there's no room for mediocre women... You have to work exceptionally hard, and you have to know what you're talking about."[97]

What I would like men to know about the challenges of being a female leader is that, because there are so many fewer of us out there, it is considerably harder to be considered a good leader. Being a female leader requires you to put up with a lot of extremely personal and unwarranted criticism and/ or abuse; to work twice as hard to be considered even equally competent as a man; to know what you are talking about all the time because your competence is often questioned; and to always look photo-ready because, apparently, our physical appearance is a distraction. I think that the presidential race between Hillary Clinton and Donald Trump clearly exemplifies this point.

There are only a handful of women leaders in the world. We need more of them because the more of us that there are, the less likely we are to be judged on issues outside of our intelligence or competence. Having appreciable numbers of women in leadership, a critical mass, needs to be the new normal. The world is wising up to the importance of having women in leadership. Rwanda is leading the way globally in terms of having female representation in Parliament. South Africa is also doing very well.

My journey has been a long and challenging one. I'm certainly not a perfect leader; there are in fact many areas in which I could improve, not least of which is managing people better. But I think the one thing that stands me in good stead is that I have been knocked down several times but refuse to get knocked out. I want to live life on my own terms, do what I think is right, and try to uplift others, particularly women, where I can. I would like to believe that I have learnt some useful lessons along the way, and these are some of them:

1. Have the courage of your convictions

For me, my faith steers me in the right direction or keeps me going when things get rough. I cannot do without it. As the Bible says, "I can do all things through Christ Jesus who strengthens me." It's where I derive my self-belief. But whatever your source of courage, be steadfast. Another thing I would say is that as a woman with an independent mind in a position of influence, it's not hard to be labelled as being "difficult". Comedian, producer, and author Amy Poehler once said, "I just love bossy women. I could be around them all day. To me, bossy is not a pejorative term at all. It means somebody's passionate and engaged and ambitious and doesn't mind leading."[98] When I read it, I thought to myself, yup that's me, and I'm just going to have to make peace with that.

2. Respect yourself

Everybody has an inviolable line, a line that no one should cross. You'll know when that line is being crossed when someone makes you uncomfortable because they are violating your values and what you stand for. Don't let anyone cross that line. Depending on the circumstances, either stand your ground or walk away.

3. Don't settle

Life is too short to be living a life of what ifs. Or as Chimamanda Ngozi Adichie puts it in her book *Americanah*,[99] what you don't want to do is be in a comfortable house and spend all your time looking outside the window to see if something better will come along. Identify what you want in life and go for it.

4. Find out what your purpose is and live it

Your purpose here on earth is a very personal thing. It

depends on what your gifts and values are. Living in that space just feels right such that when the storms in life come, you are unmoved because you know you are exactly where you are meant to be.

5. Ask

Some of the most life-changing moments in my life have come because I mustered up the courage to ask for an opportunity. You'd be surprised; people will often say yes.

6. Don't limit yourself

"There's going to be enough people in the world who will try to limit what you do. Don't limit yourself." – Lorraine Wagner

I have learnt that no one understands your full potential except you and your Maker. Often you can achieve what you believe you can do, so take calculated risks.

7. Pay it forward

As told in the Biblical parable of the faithful servant, "To whom much is given, much will be expected." My favourite parable in the Bible is in Matthew 25 verses 14-30 in the English Standard version, which is worth setting out here:

[14] "For it will be like a man going on a journey, who called his servants[a] and entrusted to them his property. [15] To one he gave five talents,[b] to another two, to another one, to each according to his ability. Then he went away. [16] He who had received the five talents went at once and traded with them, and he made five talents more. [17] So also, he who had the two talents made two talents more. [18] But he who had received the one talent went and dug in the ground and hid his master's money. [19] Now after a long time the master of those servants came and settled accounts with them. [20] And he who had received the five talents came forward, bringing five talents more, saying, 'Master, you delivered to me five talents; here, I have made five talents more.' [21] His master said to him, 'Well done, good and faithful servant.[c] You have been faithful over a little; I will set you over much. Enter into the joy of your master.' [22] And he also who had the two talents came forward, saying, 'Master, you delivered to me two talents; here, I have made two talents more.' [23] His master said to him, 'Well done, good and faithful servant. You have been faithful over a little; I will set you over much. Enter into the joy of your master.' [24] He also who had received the one talent came forward, saying, 'Master, I knew you to be a hard man, reaping where you did not sow, and gathering where you scattered no seed, [25] so I was afraid, and I

went and hid your talent in the ground. Here, you have what is yours.' [26] But his master answered him, 'You wicked and slothful servant! You knew that I reap where I have not sown and gather where I scattered no seed? [27] Then you ought to have invested my money with the bankers, and at my coming I should have received what was my own with interest. [28] So take the talent from him and give it to him who has the ten talents. [29] For to everyone who has will more be given, and he will have an abundance. But from the one who has not, even what he has will be taken away. [30]"

8. Never give up!

Zambian music producer Chali Mulalami said in a Facebook post, "The [un]exceptional rejoice when the great fall because it releases them from the burden of believing that they too can be great." Any kind of success requires risk-taking and you won't always be successful. Some people will be incredibly happy to see you meet with failure but, in those moments, you have to dig deep to discover what you're really made of. Get up! If only to drive the haters crazy.

9. Character v Reputation

John Wooden, a famous US basketball coach, once said, "Be more concerned with your character than your reputation, because your character is what you really are, while your reputation is merely what others think you are." As Romans 5:4 says, "Endurance produces character and character produces hope." There have been many times when I have wanted to throw in the towel because carrying on just seemed too hard. This often happens when I feel that I am doing my best to do the right thing and my intentions are misconstrued or misunderstood. At these times, it is important to pause and reflect on why you're doing what you're doing and what your ultimate goal is. My decision often comes down to whether I want to please man or please God.

10. Take care of yourself

Just as advised by flight attendants, in times of crisis, if you don't take care of yourself first, you will have nothing left to give. I have learnt this the hard way having experienced burnout. The toll it takes on you and those around you is just not worth it. There is a difference between getting rest and being replenished. You need both. Pioneer play researcher Dr. Brian Sutton-Smith said,

> *"The opposite of play is not work – the opposite of play is depression… Respecting our biologically programmed need for play can transform work. It can bring back excitement and newness to our job.*

> *Play helps us deal with difficulties, provides a sense of expansiveness, promotes mastery of our craft, and is an essential part of the creative process. Most important, true play that comes from our own inner needs and desires is the only path to finding lasting joy and satisfaction in our work. In the long run, work does not work without play."*[100]

As Oprah Winfrey likes to say, make sure your cup "runneth over".

By virtue of our different experiences due to our gender, women bring a different perspective to the table. In my view, courage, perseverance, and a good dose of self-belief are the key to being successful. For me, my faith plays an important part in everything that I do. On your own, you are too small to think that you can win a battle with Goliath or escape the lions' den unscathed. Ultimately, as the very clever Zambian wordsmith Chanda Mfula put it in another Facebook post, "At the conclusion of every story of public service, only integrity survives."

In summary, being a woman in leadership is hard. But it will only get better when more women step forward to accept the challenge. Aspiring for leadership can be a noble pursuit. The writer Maya Angelou once said, "If one is lucky, a solitary fantasy can totally transform one million realities."[101]

EPILOGUE:

TAKING OUR POWER BACK

"There's no use in having power if you don't use it, and if you're not aware of it, and if you're afraid. There's no use in having power if you don't understand it, and you won't let others know that you have the courage to use it.[102]"

– Mikki Taylor

In 2015, I took my first real vacation in three years. I had steadily been climbing the rungs of leadership both at the law firm at which I was a named partner and in "legal politics" within the governing structures of the national Bar Association. I did not go to an exotic location but, for the first time in a really long time, I decided to "vacate" the official labels attached to my name and rediscover who I am and what makes me tick. A few weeks previously, I had bought a large TV stand for my almost-new TV that was sitting on a piece of furniture that I had inherited from my parents. The new TV stand had been sitting in a big box against a wall right next to my old makeshift one. I was waiting for my brother, Mutale, or "someone" to help me unpack it, put it in its new place and reconnect the TV and decoder that I wanted to put on it.

One day during my vacation, I decided that I would be the "someone" who would unpack the box and put everything in its place. After a couple of hours of de-cluttering and heavy lifting, it was done. I was beaming proudly; that wasn't so bad after all. It was actually liberating. I sent a text message to a few friends bragging about my accomplishment saying, "Here's to showing up in your own life!" Perhaps my friends did not truly grasp the significance of this small feat, but for me it has been life changing.

There are thousands of ways in which we give away our own power every day. So many times, we wait for someone to make us happy, to validate us, to help us make personal decisions that we already have the answers to, or to give us permission to simply be who we are. That is extremely disempowering. On the day that I managed to assemble my TV stand, I opened my devotional Bible and the page I turned to contained a poem by Madeleine L'Engle[103] which says:

> *"The most difficult thing to let go is myself, that self which, coddled and cozened, becomes smaller as it becomes heavier. I don't understand how and why I come to be only as I lose myself, but I know from long experience that this is so."*

How true those words are. We really are the greatest stumbling blocks in our own lives. Sometimes we just need to get out of our own way. A while ago I was in a meeting and asked for volunteers to carry out an assignment. The only two other women in the meeting opted out, stating that they did not think they had the necessary skills to do the job. A few days later, I called one of them out on it. "Lean in!" I told her. She responded that, actually, she did not have a problem leaning in, but was still considering what direction to take in the organization. I told her I was glad that she did not have a problem leaning in but asked her to consider the chapter in the book *Lean In* that says, "Don't leave until you leave."[104] In that chapter Sheryl Sandberg narrates how a young woman in her twenties approached her for tips on work-life balance. She told Sandberg that she was considering cutting back at work because she wanted to make room for a husband and children. Upon further inquiry it turned out that the young woman wasn't even in a relationship at the time and yet she was already giving away her power.

As women, it's so easy to give our power away. It's nice to be "coddled and cozened" sometimes, but I think that if the price of constantly succumbing to that causes us to lose ourselves in the process, then it is a price too dear to pay. We each have our own journey of self-discovery. I acknowledge that I may have to keep reminding myself of my small victory over the years to remain liberated, but I know that the potential rewards are limitless. So, here's to taking our power back!

Acknowledgements

I would like to thank my mum, my sister, and my brother for standing by me and supporting me through the most difficult of times. I love you guys! I would like to thank my friend Laura Miti for being a great listening ear and for reviewing several drafts of the book and giving me very thoughtful feedback. I would like to thank my friends Natasha Chiumya, Ntombenhle Khathwane, and Mubanga Kalimamukwento for reading the earlier drafts of the book and cheering me on. Thanks also to Tshepo Shabangu for being a shoulder to lean on. Thank you to my editor Elizabeth Ridley for her helpful comments. And last but not least, thank you to my dear Nkabika for your love and support.

Endnotes

Chapter One: It Matters How It Starts

1 Film released on 2nd March 1965, music composed by Richard Rodgers, Oscar Hammerstein, and Irwin Kostal.

2 By Billi P.S. Lim, published by Hard Knocks Factory, 2007.

3 Episode 14 Beyoncé/Sheryl Sandberg Copyright © 2013 CNN Newsource Sales Inc.

4 *Nelson Mandela: Prisoner to President* documentary, 1994, directed by Peter Davis.

5 https://eliasmunshya.org/2015/03/21/wrong-general-linda-kasondes-opposition-to-appointment-of-likando-kalaluka-as-attorney-general/.

6 *Lean In: Women, Work, and the Will to Lead* by Sheryl Sandberg and Nell Scovell, 2013. Published by Alfred A. Knopf at page 38.

7 Kathleen McGinn and Nicole Tempest, *Heidi Rozen,* Harvard Business School Case Study #9-800-228 (Boston: Harvard Business School Publishing, 2009).

8 https://web.facebook.com/RobinSharmaOfficial/photos/sometimes-youll-be-the-only-one-who-believes-in-your-dream-do-not-stop-the-world/10153663033445040/?paipv=0&eav=AfbgRjGETWO0R15-HPC9qfJR9qYpsrS2b-AmitmbbrSoeglSs-Chk6xJdHV_A5hU-Xck&_rdc=1&_rdr.

Chapter Two: "The Iron Lady"

9 Margaret Thatcher's speech to the Conservative Party Conference, 10th October 1980.
10 https://allafrica.com/stories/201606290554.html
11 https://www.unicef.org/zambia/children-zambia#:~:text=The%20maternal%20mortality%20ratio%20declined,deaths%20per%201%2C000%20live%20births.
12 https://reliefweb.int/report/zambia/how-zambia-has-reduced-maternal-deaths-300-cent-16-years
13 https://www.unicef.org/zambia/children-zambia#:~:text=The%20maternal%20mortality%20ratio%20declined,deaths%20per%201%2C000%20live%20births.
14 https://data.worldbank.org/indicator/SP.DYN.TFRT.IN?locations=ZM.

Chapter Three: The Quest to Save Zambia's Democracy

15 https://www.washingtonpost.com/archive/politics/1990/07/01/coup-attempt-foiled-against-zambian-leader/22b22e07-a1bb-41b0-99c3-4663ba9d5744/.
16 https://www.washingtonpost.com/archive/politics/1990/06/29/calm-returns-to-zambia-after-3-days-of-riots/a5ba094d-f118-4bdf-a140-5838d35d841f/.
17 https://muse.jhu.edu/article/225530/summary.
18 http://saipar.org/wp-content/uploads/2015/12/Political-and-Economic-Liberalisation-in-Zambia_Lise-Rakner.pdf.
19 https://link.springer.com/chapter/10.1007/978-3-030-40810-7_7.
20 https://www.tandfonline.com/doi/abs/10.1080/03057070.2020.1730644?needAccess=true&journalCode=cjss20.

21 https://www.news24.com/news24/mwanawasa-wins-by-a-whisker-20020102.
22 https://www.voanews.com/a/a-13-a-2001-12-29-19-zambia-66439607/550751.html.
23 https://www.thenewhumanitarian.org/news/2005/02/17/supreme-court-upholds-mwanawasas-election.
24 https://www.reuters.com/article/us-zambia-corruption-chiluba-idUSTRE57G3N320090817.
25 https://www.theguardian.com/world/2008/aug/19/zambia.
26 https://www.sardc.net/en/southern-african-news-features/rupiah-banda-wins-zambias-fourth-presidential-election/.
27 https://www.dandc.eu/en/article/after-tough-rhetoric-election-campaign-zambias-new-president-sata-must-cooperate-chinese.
28 https://www.researchgate.net/profile/Kelvin-Mambwe/publication/361470700_Political_Discourses_in_a_Multiparty_Democracy_The_Case_of_Dandy_Krazy's_Donchi_Kubeba/links/62b362a3d49f803365b183df/Political-Discourses-in-a-Multiparty-Democracy-The-Case-of-Dandy-Krazys-Donchi-Kubeba.pdf.
29 https://www.bbc.com/news/av/world-africa-15035741.
30 https://mg.co.za/article/2011-09-23-zambias-king-cobra-sata-sworn-in-as-president/.
31 https://www.reuters.com/article/zambia-sata-idUSL5E7LE1LO20111014.
32 https://www.aljazeera.com/news/2014/10/29/zambias-president-michael-sata-dies.
33 https://library.au.int/white-man-will-never-be-zambian-racialised-nationalism-rule-law-and-competing-visions-independent.
34 https://www.nytimes.com/2014/12/19/world/africa/guy-scott-zambia-elections.html.

35 https://www.bbc.com/news/world-africa-30970952.
36 https://www.voanews.com/a/zambia-new-president-sworn-into-office/2612565.html.
37 https://media.zambialii.org/files/judgments/zmcc/2017/7/2017-zmcc-7.pdf.
38 http://saipar.org/wp-content/uploads/2013/09/Ndulo_Law-Association-of-Zambia-Annual-Meeting_Judicial-Reform-Constitutionalism-and-the-Rule-of-Law-in-Zambia.pdf.
39 https://diggers.news/local/2017/11/02/lungu-says-there-will-be-chaos-if-judges-disqualify-him-for-2021/.
40 https://allafrica.com/stories/201612030029.html.
41 https://www.lusakatimes.com/2017/03/21/pf-take-bill-parliament-kill-laz/.

Chapter Four: Impeachment

42 *Reel to Real: Race, Class, and Sex at the Movies* by bell hooks, published by Routledge, 1996.
43 https://slate.com/human-interest/2017/03/what-happens-when-the-worlds-few-female-leaders-get-impeached.html
44 https://diggers.news/local/2017/02/18/mmembe-laments-wifes-arrest/.
45 (1998) SJ 26 (S.C)
46 Statutory Instrument No. 51 of 2002.
47 https://allafrica.com/stories/201704250836.html.
48 https://diggers.news/local/2017/04/27/kbf-escalates-anti-linda-campaign-as-research-implicates-lungu/.
49 https://diggers.news/local/2017/04/28/kbf-sues-laz-over-impeachment-procedure/.
50 https://www.latimes.com/world/la-fg-zambia-opposition-treason-2017-htmlstory.html.
51 https://www.reuters.com/article/us-zambia-politics-idUSKCN1AW0KZ.

52 https://www.aljazeera.com/news/2017/9/8/tanzanias-tundu-lissu-recovering-after-gun-attack.
53 https://pmrczambia.com/presidential-speech-to-parliament-on-the-state-of-the-nation-infographic-2017/.
54 https://slate.com/human-interest/2017/03/what-happens-when-the-worlds-few-female-leaders-get-impeached.html.

Chapter Five: Power and Vulnerability

55 https://www.who.int/news/item/28-05-2019-burn-out-an-occupational-phenomenon-international-classification-of-diseases.
56 https://www.hrw.org/news/2023/01/25/eswatini-activist-rights-lawyer-brutally-killed.
57 https://www.frontlinedefenders.org/en/case/zambian-hrd-pilato-arrested-during-youth-forum-laura-miti-bornwell-mwewa-arrested-when.
58 https://oslofreedomforum.com/speakers/thulani-maseko/.
59 *The Gifts of Imperfection: Let Go of Who You Think You're Supposed to Be and Embrace Who You Are*, by Dr. Brené Brown, Hazelden Publishers, 27th August 2010.
60 *The Works of Robert G. Ingersoll,* by Robert G. Ingersoll, Volume 3 of 12, Dresden Edition Lectures, 1900.
61 https://www.oprah.com/inspiration/life-lessons-we-all-need-to-learn-brene-brown.
62 https://www.oprahdaily.com/entertainment/tv-movies/a27195228/brene-brown-netflix-call-to-courage-vulnerability-review/.

Chapter Six: Battling Goliath

63 *David and Goliath: Underdogs, Misfits, and the Art of*

Battling Giants, by Malcolm Gladwell, published by Little, Brown and Company, 1st October 2013.

64 https://www.themastonline.com/linda-kasonde-elected-commonwealth-lawyers-association-vice-president-for-africa-2/.

65 *Twilight of the Idols*, by Friedrich Nietzsche, first published in 1889, recently published by Hacket Publishing Company Inc, 1st June 1997.

66 Quoted in *Unexpected News: Reading the Bible with Third World Eyes,* by Robert McAfee Brown, published by Westminster John Knox Press, First Edition 1st January 1984.

67 *The Alchemist,* by Paulo Coelho, published by HarperOne, First Edition, 25th April 2006.

68 https://www.youtube.com/watch?v=cY0nvLUfC_o.

69 https://www.parliament.gov.zm/node/8067.

70 https://www.aljazeera.com/news/2017/4/12/upnd-leader-hakainde-hichilema-charged-with-treason.

71 https://www.aljazeera.com/news/2017/4/12/upnd-leader-hakainde-hichilema-charged-with-treason.

72 https://diggers.news/local/2019/09/07/yellow-card-campaign-goes-south/.

73 https://www.lusakatimes.com/2019/11/20/linda-kasonde-saddened-with-the-lack-of-interest-by-zambians-in-the-petition-against-bill-number-10/.

74 https://diggers.news/courts/2019/11/30/think-of-future-generations-as-you-vote-on-bill-10-mwitwa-implores-mps/.

75 https://www.africanews.com/2020/10/30/zambia-s-ruling-party-s-controversial-bid-to-pass-bill-10-fails//.

76 https://diggers.news/courts/2021/06/09/sangwa-arguments-in-the-constitutional-court-against-edgar-lungus-eligibility/.

77 https://www.lusakatimes.com/2021/06/11/constitutional-

court-declares-patriotic-front-presidential-candidate-edgar-lungu-eligible-for-august-12-polls/.

78 https://allafrica.com/stories/202108150063.html.

79 *Born a Crime: Stories from a South African Childhood,* by Trevor Noah, published by One World, 15th November 2016 at page 73.

80 https://www.youtube.com/watch?v=M038O7bN6ko.

Chapter Seven: Friendly Fire

81 This was featured in her *My Day* column for the United Features Syndicate in 1937.

82 https://diggers.news/courts/2020/08/07/chapter-one-drags-ecz-to-concourt-over-30-days-voter-registration-exercise/.

83 https://diggers.news/diggers-lite/2021/01/27/class-of-2020-zambians-who-gravely-disappointed-last-year/.

84 https://diggers.news/diggers-lite/2021/01/27/class-of-2020-zambians-who-gravely-disappointed-last-year/.

85 https://diggers.news/guest-diggers/2021/01/29/response-to-dr-sishuwa-sishuwas-critique-of-ms-linda-kasondes-2020-performance/.

86 https://diggers.news/guest-diggers/2021/02/15/i-respect-and-appreciate-linda-kasonde-but-she-messed-up-big-time-here-is-why/.

87 https://www.elections.org.zm/2021-general-election-results-and-statistics/.

88 https://www.znbc.co.zm/news/ecz-told-to-start-continuous-voter-registration/.

89 https://diggers.news/local/2022/02/18/weve-already-planned-for-continuous-voter-registration-ecz/.

90 https://diggers.news/opinion/2022/06/01/continuous-voter-registration-must-be-made-available-online/.

91 https://www.lusakatimes.com/2016/01/11/is-african-

culture-killing-our-race/.
92 Ibid *Born a Crime: Stories of a South African Childhood* at page 143.

Chapter Eight: Women, Resilience, and the Will to Lead

93 https://www.forbesafrica.com/politics/2012/08/01/the-struggle-continues/.
94 https://www.youtube.com/watch?v=5TLFhUhj82o.
95 https://www.nytimes.com/2016/10/02/opinion/sunday/ruth-bader-ginsburgs-advice-for-living.html.
96 Ibid.
97 https://www.forbes.com/sites/francesbridges/2015/06/24/what-madeline-albright-wants-women-to-know/?sh=3f4104ee3063.
98 https://www.glamour.com/story/amy-poehler-tells-katie-couric-i-just-love-bossy-women.
99 *Americanah,* by Chimamanda Ngozi Adichie, published by Vintage, 4th March 2014.
100 Cited by Dr. Brené Brown in *The Gifts of Imperfection.*
101 *The Heart of a Woman,* by Maya Angelou, published by Random House, 17th May 1997.

Epilogue: Taking Our Power Back

102 https://www.essence.com/lifestyle/black-girl-magic/mikki-taylor-reflects-why-her-time-essence-was-epitome-blackgirlmagic/.
103 From her memoir, *The Irrational Season,* published by HarperOne, 1st January 1977.
104 Ibid Chapter 7 *Lean In.*

https://lindakasonde.com/

Printed in Great Britain
by Amazon

41790821R00111